THE STATE OF THE LIBRARY ART

the state of the library art

edited by Ralph R. Shaw

volume 5, part 1

Production of Micro-Forms

by

Reginald Hawkins

GREENWOOD PRESS, PUBLISHERS
WESTPORT, CONNECTICUT

Library of Congress Cataloging in Publication Data

Hawkins, Reginald.
Production of micro-forms.

Reprint of the 1960 ed. published by Graduate School of Library Service, Rutgers, the State University, New Brunswick, N. J., which was issued as v. 5, pt. 1 of The State of the library art.
Bibliography: p.
Includes index.
1. Microforms. 2. Microphotography. 3. Photography—Library applications. I. Title. II. Series: The State of the library art ; v. 5, pt. 1.
[Z265.H34 1975] 686.4'3 75-17838
ISBN 0-8371-8235-2

This volume is one of a series of studies in librarianship published by the Graduate School of Library Service * Rutgers- The State University and distributed by the Rutgers University Press

Originally published in 1960 by the Graduate School of Library Service, Rutgers-The State University, New Brunswick, N.J.

Reprinted with the permission of Rutgers University Press

Reprinted in 1975 by Greenwood Press, a division of Williamhouse-Regency Inc.

Library of Congress Catalog Card Number 75-17838

ISBN 0-8371-8235-2

Printed in the United States of America

Preface

Pierce Butler planted the seed of this work some thirty years ago when he attempted to persuade me to follow my translation of Georg Schneider's "Theory and History of Bibliography" with an English rendering of Milkau's "Handbuch der Bibliothekswissenschaft." As we discussed this in his cubbyhole at the University of Chicago it became increasingly apparent that for all the excellence and usefulness of the Milkau, a version in English would require such wide revision and additions as to constitute a completely new work, and the project was, I thought, abandoned. Over the years, however, it remained a subject of, perhaps sometimes subconscious, dreaming, thinking, and occasionally some work.

When the Council on Library Resources was organized its need for information on the state of the library art resulted in almost spontaneous germination of Pierce Butler's long dormant seed. This resulted in a grant to the Graduate School of Library Service at Rutgers for preparation under the direction of the undersigned, of a review of the status of our current knowledge of librarianship. From the inception of this project it was recognized that the initial grant could cover only somewhat less than half of the vast field, and there are many areas of librarianship still to be covered.

An advisory committee helped in the design of the program and in determining priorities for treatment of the various aspects of the field.

The advisory committee included: Dr. Julian H. Bigelow, Institute for Advanced Study at Princeton, New Jersey, Mr. Verner W. Clapp, President of the Council on Library Resources, Mr. Donald Coney, Librarian of the University of California, Mr. J. W. Kuipers, Apparatus research and development in Itek Corporation, Dr. Robert D. Leigh, Dean of the School of Library Service at Columbia University, Dr. Lowell A. Martin, Dean of the Graduate School of Library Service at Rutgers, Professor A. J. Riker of the College of

Agriculture at the University of Wisconsin, Dr. Melville J. Ruggles, Vice-president of the Council on Library Resources, Mr. A. N. Sears, Vice-president of Remington Rand, and Dr. Eugene H. Wilson, Vice-president of the University of Colorado.

Since the volumes now completed and being prepared for publication cover perhaps forty percent of the entire range of librarianship and bibliography, the plan of publication is in the familiar "Handbuch" form so as to permit the addition of volumes as financial resources and dedicated writers become available.

The organization of the series in various stages of production are tentatively as follows:

Volume One -- Technical Service
- Part 1. Cataloging, by Maurice F. Tauber.
- Part 2. Classification, by Maurice F. Tauber and Edith Wise, Coding, by Doralyn Hickey, and Subject Heading, by Carlyle Frarey.
- Part 3. Acquisition, Gifts and Exchanges, by Helen J. Harrar and Ronald Watterson, Donald F. Thompson and others.

Volume Two -- Reader Services
- Part 1. Training layment in use of the library, by George H. Bonn.
- Part 2. Bibliographical services, by Margaret S. Bryant.
- Part 3. Charging systems, by Lila H. Kirkwood.

Volume Three -- Storage of Library Materials
- Part 1. Buildings, by Ralph E. Ellsworth, Shelving, by Louis Kaplan, and Storage warehouses, by Jerrold Orne.

Volume Four -- Retrieval Systems
- Part 1. Punched cards, by Ralph Blasingame and Electronic searching, by Gerald Jehoda.
- Part 2. Notched cards, by Felix Reichman and Peekaboo cards by Lawrence S. Thompson.

Volume Five -- Reproduction of Materials
- Part 1. Production of microforms, Reginald Hawkins.
- Part 2. Reading Devices, by Jean Stewart.
- Part 3. Production of full-size copies, by William Hawken.

It is hoped that all of the above will be in print before the end of 1960. In preparing these for publication it appeared best to permit some variations in style from one volume to another rather than to devote a large percentage of our resources to achieving a standard style for all.

The general pattern followed in these studies consists of a survey of the published and unpublished literature of each facet of the field. In this survey, as a first step, each compiler attempts to summarize what the literature says with a minimum of redundancy but without editorial comment. Each statement is accompanied by a footnote so that investigation in depth can be conducted when necessary, but for most purposes, if we have adequately performed our primary task, it should be unnecessary to search the literature for information on the topics covered. A second step, provided in most cases, is the examination of the evidence provided to support each allegation or statement in the literature and an indication of whether that particular bit of "the art" is empirical or the extent and reliability of the objective data provided to support it.

This pattern of presentation is modified in a number of the parts of the series since, except for the sake of external uniformity, it would serve little purpose to repeat substantially every statement in this second part followed by the words, "no objective evidence."

It was initially planned to present each summary in the historical perspective of the development of its field but this method of treatment was found unsuitable for some of the subjects. In some cases, such as the study of "Reading Devices for Micro-Images," both historical and topical treatments are presented; in others the treatment is historical only, and in still others primary emphasis is given to topical treatment. Here as in the review of evidence, suitability for each topic is given priority over external uniformity of the set.

While a few of these reports were prepared by staff assistants, as indicated by the list of titles and research staff given above, we were fortunate in enlisting participants of outstanding authority and reputation in most of the subject areas treated. In most cases the resultant first draft was read by one or more additional specialists in the field and in this work we had the assistance of such well known authorities as: Hubbard W. Ballou, Ralph H. Carruthers, Ralph Esterquest, Robert A. Fairthorne, John Fall, Charles F. Gosnell, Lutz Helbig, Laurence Kipp, Alfred H. Lane, Chester Lewis, Calvin N. Mooers, Robert H. Muller, Maurice F. Tauber, Lawrence S. Thompson, and others.

This is the concerted work of many hands, and many more than those listed above have helped in almost countless ways. Such value as may reside in this series is the result of professional contributions of high order by many people. Final responsibility for the plan of work, selection and supervision of research staff, revision of manuscripts as well as editing them and production of the volumes rested solely on the undersigned and he accepts full responsibility for the imperfections to be found in this series. It is hoped that this review of the library art will, on balance, be found to make a useful contribution and that it may some time be carried forward to cover the whole field of librarianship.

Ralph R. Shaw

Table of Contents

History of Microcopying

Early history of microcopying. In the Athenaeum of July 9, 1853, two letters (1) were printed in which are embodied what is apparently the first suggestion of the microcopying of documentary material. One letter from John Stewart contains this paragraph:

> Should your ideas of preserving public records in a concentrated form on microscopic negatives ever be adopted, the immediate positive reproduction on an enlarged readable scale without the possibility of injury to the plate, will be of service.

The other letter, signed J. F. W. Herschel, reads in part:

> Your insertion of the annexed letter from my brother-in-law, Mr. John Stewart, of Pau, will oblige me... In reference to the concluding paragraph, I will only add, that the publication of concentrated microscopic editions of works of reference--maps, atlases, logarithmic tables, or the concentration for pocket use of private notes and MSS, &c, &c, and innumerable other similar applications is brought within reach of anyone who possesses a small achromatic object glass...and a brass tube, with slides before and behind the lens...to receive the plate.... The details...are too obvious to need mention.

At least as early as 1857, Sir David Brewster (2) suggested that documents could be reduced to microscopic form so that dispatches and other secret information could be concealed in small places. Nevertheless, the landmark name in the history of microcopying of documents is Dagron, a Paris photographer who, during the siege of Paris in 1870, reduced large numbers of messages, news items and related documents to microfilm "pellicules" so small that a single carrier pigeon was able to transport many documents at one time. There are numerous accounts of Dagron and the Pigeon Post with Frank Luther's being perhaps the most satisfactory one, particularly in view of its extensive biography (3).

In its early years, documentary microphotography was confined largely to the making of novelties most of which had the form of a paper tube with a small magnifying lens at one end and a glass slide containing the microscopic image at the opposite end. The image was viewed by holding the device up to the light and looking through the lens. Dagron published a manual describing in detail the apparatus, chemicals, and procedure for making the microscopic photographs used in these novelties (4). Descriptions of the microscopic images and techniques of producing them were written also by Willemin (5), Lefevre (6), and Fabre (7) among others.

Modern history of microcopying. The modern development of microcopying began in 1906 with the reading of a paper by Goldschmidt and Otlet (8) at the Congrès International de la Documentation Photographique in Marseilles. This paper was published the next year in the Bulletin of the International Institute of Bibliography. These authors suggested the copying of books on 7.5 x 12.5 cm. sheets of film. On a sheet or card of these dimensions they proposed to place 72 microimages, together with a title and other identifying information at the top of the card in letters large enough to be read with the unaided eye. In the same article they pointed out the space-saving potentialities of ribbon or roll film, noting that a roll of cinema film 50 meters long holds 5,000 pictures each of which can be projected to form an image with an area of 16 square meters. Such a film can be stored in a metal box 15 cm. in diameter and 2.5 cm. wide, thus making it possible to store 80,000 square meters of documentary material in this small space. However, their suggestion was not taken seriously nor its significance noted until it was renewed and republished in 1925 (9).

In the 1925 publication, Goldschmidt and Otlet called attention to their 1906 proposal and reiterated some of the details; they surveyed the potential applications under main headings such as bibliography, patents, and education; discussed projection and enlargement; and noted prices of the prototype negative and positive print, and of a negative copy of a 200-page book. Lemare invented a combination automatic camera, processor and enlarger, a specialized model of which was designed for enlarging from cinematographic film. Both models were described and illustrated in a paper by Rossignon (10). In an article on the Berthelot Centenary, Seidell (11) mentioned that the International Office of Chemistry was planning to photograph printed articles on film, the films to be sent to users who would project them for reading.

Meanwhile, George I. McCarthy, then an officer of a bank in New York City, was developing his automatic machine for the photographing of bank checks. This machine, which in 1928 was placed on the market under the trade name Recordak, was eventually to supply the impetus for the development of practical microcopying of documentary material on a large scale (1).

In 1928 and 1929 the League of Nations took notice of microfilm and its implications for documentation. In 1928 (12) the Committee of Library Experts visited the studios of the Photoscopie Company and viewed reproductions made by that company of rare artistic and literary documents. In 1929 the following resolution (13) was passed:

> That the next Committee of Library Experts should be asked to study the questions relating to facsimiles and the microphotographical publication of documents. It is understood that the Institute will first address itself to manufacturers and producers so as to be able to submit useful material for comparison to the experts.

A notice (14) of the formation of the Photoscopie firm indicates that it was based on the idea of R. Goldschmidt (9) and that its purpose was to publish reproductions of manuscripts, scarce books, etc. on moving picture film. In the same source it is indicated that plans were on foot for the installation of a reading room for microfilms at the Bibliothèque Nationale and for exchange of films with other libraries. Binkley (45) mentions (p. 162-163) a Belgian firm of the same name (the same firm?) which in the twenties issued a catalog of films of geographic, scientific and other subjects which were intended as substitutes for glass slides used in visual education and a similar enterprise, the Cinescopie, located in Brussels.

Microcopying by individual scholars of books, manuscripts and archival material developed gradually and sporadically. Johnson's (175) experiences, though possibly not typical, do describe the scholar's approach to the problem in this period. When the Leica camera became available, many individual scholars adopted it for microcopying, and a paper (15) on its use in copying from books appeared in 1930. Binkley (16) appraised microfilm as a low-cost method of reproducing research materials. A major project of copying in Europe of materials relating to American history by the Library of Congress using an EKA Lemare camera and special copying stand attracted the notice of a daily newspaper (17). Henry (18) in an article on film copies in libraries discussed costs, film dimensions, cameras, projectors, and storage of films from the librarian's point of view.

However, documentary microphotography had not assumed sufficient importance to attract the attention of Eder when he was writing the comprehensive fourth edition of his history of photography (19). His discussion of microphotography mentions Dancer, Dagron, and other early workers in the field, but gives no account of the beginnings of present-day microcopying as such.

Bendikson's significant experiments with microprints on paper were the subject of a short account in the 1932/33 annual report of the Henry E. Huntington Library and Art Gallery and of a longer article in a professional journal (20). Bendikson described methods of making and reading reduced prints of rare and valuable books reproduced on paper from film negatives. Articles providing general and semi-technical information on the preservation of newspaper files on microfilm appeared in journalism trade journals (21, 22).

Although considerable copying on film had been done by 1933 in the United States of America, especially for some of the large research libraries, only five libraries, Harvard University, Yale University, Library of Congress, Henry E. Huntington Library and Art Gallery, and the William L. Clements Library were prepared to accept orders for film copies (23). Even these libraries were not yet filling orders in large numbers. Some were merely offering enlargements from films in their collections, although the Library of Congress reported that it was prepared to furnish negative copies on film of any material in the library. Yale University Library reported that its film business for one year consisted of 21 orders for a total of 2,279 openings, or about 4,000 pages.

In a discussion of reduced scale copying published in 1934, Binkley (24) proposed the installation of a camera for copying on film in the Library of Congress to supply microfilm copies in lieu of interlibrary loan, and he pointed out some of the advantages of transparent film over opaque paper. However, microfilm was considered as only one of a number of schemes for reduced scale copying. Brown (25), writing in the Library journal, described in a tentative fashion the experiment then in progress in the New York Public Library with newspapers on microfilm; and Henry (26) commented editorially on the experiment in a way that leaves no doubt about its being the first of the kind.

The work of Georges Sébille was described by Otlet (27) in 1934. Sébille, looking toward the eventual development of an automatic catalog, the cards of which would be microcopied on film, invented and patented a roll microfilm system in which the documents were copied at a 1:20 reduction ratio and which embodied a system for making page numbers visible as the film unrolled in the machine. French patents 673,365 and 696,287 were issued on Sébille's inventions. Microphotography on paper is discussed briefly in the same article. Otlet's treatise (28) on photography contains a short discussion of microfilm and its applications to documentation with a survey of the contemporary status of apparatus and forms of microcopy.

Kimberley and Scribner (29) in a summary report of National Bureau of Standards research devoted most of their attention to methods of record preservation other than microcopying. In a short section on preservation by reproduction, they mentioned a number of characteristics of film and film emulsions which seemed to indicate that even cellulose acetate film was not a suitable material for preservation of records. In concluding this discussion, they stated: "It...appears that more permanent reproductions may be obtained by the use of photostats than by the use of filmslides or similar methods." However, Scribner (30), in another paper summarizing National Bureau of Standards research on newspaper preservation, reported that the technique of preserving newspaper records on microfilm appeared to be an ideal way of preserving them, and that the making of such photographs and projecting them for reading had reached a satisfactory state of development.

Bendikson (31) surveyed microprints on paper, photostats (economy photostats) and microfilm from the viewpoint of their usefulness in the reproduction of rare, unique works, fragile books, documents, etc. and argued for the superiority of paper. In the same article he discussed briefly the use of photographic techniques in producing copies of stained, defaced and faded materials which are more legible than the originals.

In 1934-35, van Asperen (32), surveying new developments in photographic reproduction from a European viewpoint, devoted most of his space to methods other than microcopying, but did discuss the latter. In 1935, the implications of microfilm and related methods of low-cost copying and publication were already clear enough to justify an article by Binkley (33) in which these developments were discussed for "men of letters." Nevertheless, microfilm copying was viewed as still very much in the experimental stage by Case (34) who discussed methods, materials and equipment with particular reference to Recordak machines.

The fields of application of microcopies on paper and on film were discussed by Duyvis (35), who favored paper over film. Duyvis's article appeared in the proceedings of a conference on the role of film in documentation held under the auspices of the Office International de Chimie, an event which clearly indicated that users of document copies were at least abreast of librarians in appraising the usefulness of microfilm. In the same collection of proceedings, Gillot (36) discussed in a semi-technical manner such problems as reduction, enlargement, and readability of microcopies on 35 mm. film. Johnson (37) described extensive experiences in the copying of books and manuscripts in European libraries with a small 35 mm. camera. In the same paper he discussed film, costs of contact printing, and enlarging from the individual scholar's viewpoint.

The question of whether the time had arrived to preserve newspapers on film was put to a number of leading libraries and experts by Kuhlman (38), who summarized the replies, many of which pointed up unsettled questions such as the durability of microfilm. Seidell (39) discussed in several journals the microcopying on film of periodical articles, and outlined the development of microfilm in the United States of America, including the establishment of the Bibliofilm Service in the Library of the United States Department of Agriculture. Tate (40) outlined the beginnings of documentary microcopying in the use of photography in facsimile reproduction and direct copying on paper negatives (photostat), then in the same article described microfilm, its advantages for scholars, and the equipment then available for library microcopying.

Bibliofilm Service of the United States Department of Agriculture sent out its first microfilm copies on November 15, 1934. When a little more than a year's experience had been accumulated, Barnett (41) wrote an article describing the beginning of the Service, its purposes, its equipment, and giving statistics on the number of users and numbers of articles and pages copied during the year. Bendikson (42) described microcopying activities at the Henry E. Huntington Library and Art Gallery and put in another plea for microcopies on paper in Microphotography for libraries, 1936, the first of two symposium volumes sponsored by the American Library Association to inform librarians generally about microcopying. Carruthers (43) compared microfilm and 70 mm. photographic paper and found some advantages to the paper in supplying low-reduction copies to scholars. Davis (44) authoritatively described the origin and activities in microphotography of the Documentation Division of Science Service, particularly its program for the development of new machines and its experimental operation of Bibliofilm Service and Publication Service.

Microfilming and other methods of reduced-scale copying were thoroughly described and compared from the standpoint of their usefulness in the reproduction of research materials by Binkley (45) in the second edition of his important Manual. Metcalf (46) wrote a broad survey of microcopying in the United States of America, covering its early development; events during 1935; the chief problems awaiting solution and a proposal for a non-profit corporation with a revolving fund to undertake microfilming on a large scale. The advantages of microfilm over glass photographic plates were discussed by Patterson (47) who also pointed out that photography had been used, chiefly to make lantern slides, in Armstrong College Library as early as 1893.

The problems of film widths, frame sizes, perforations, image positions, etc., were critically examined by Pratt (48), who although recognizing the need for eventual standardization, at least in some degree, voiced a warning against too early standardization. Under the title "Microphotography notes" (49), the Committee on Photographic Reproduction of Library Materials of the American Library Association began publication in the Association's Bulletin of a column to record developments in microfilming and equipment for microfilming. Microcopying of documents was presented to specialists in motion picture photography by Schellenberg (50) who sketched its history and explained its advantages.

The National Bureau of Standards (51) recommended the adoption of two film widths, 16 mm. and 35 mm. Film reproductions produced by the Photographic Division of the Library of Congress were mentioned for the first time in the Report of the librarian (52). A practical method of photographing nine book openings on a 13 x 18 cm. photographic plate, which after developing was used to produce positive prints on paper, was developed by van Iterson (53). Saint Rat (54) was the author of a general survey of the state of microfilm in documentation. His paper includes a description and pictures of the S.R.S. camera developed by the author and Seidell.

Because 1936, which saw the publication of Microphotography for libraries, 1936 (64) and the second edition of Binkley's Manual (45), marks a turning point in the acceptance of microcopying as a practical library technique, this narration of the steps in its historical development will not be carried beyond this year. Only clear-cut historical articles are mentioned in the remainder of this section of this report. Running developments after 1936 are noted under appropriate headings in other sections.

A condensed history of the International Federation for Documentation by Duyvis (55) contains much information on the development of microphotography in European countries and on the activities of the Federation and its predecessor, the International Institute of Bibliography, in the furthering of microcopy. The high points in the development and application of microfilming to library use in the United States of America to 1940 were pointed out by Fussler (56). An outstanding historical account by Tate (57) appeared in a cyclopedia of photography.

Pollard (58) showed that the production of miniature documents had extended back at least to ancient Nineveh and cited numerous instances of diminutive handwriting and printing, while covering also the development of present-day microcopying. Technical aspects are emphasized in a historical review primarily of developments in Great Britain and France by Stevens (59). Dagron's pioneer exploitation of the potentialities of microcopying in communication at a distance is the subject of a definitive article by Luther (3) who also wrote a well-documented account (60) of the beginnings of microcopying.

Microcopying (In General)

The organization of the Documentation Division of Science Service was a major step in the placing of microcopying for documentation purposes on a solid footing. Davis (44) gives an account of the efforts which began in 1925 and eventually culminated in a grant from the Chemical Foundation to support the development of suitable mechanisms. He discusses also the experimental establishment of two services, the Bibliofilm Service started in cooperation with the Library of the United States Department of Agriculture, and the Auxilliary Publication Service operated in cooperation with scientific journals. The contemporary status of microcopying is outlined and the mechanisms under development are listed.

Schellenberg (50), addressing motion picture engineers, enumerated these advantages of microphotographic duplication for research workers: reduction of bulk, permanence of film, easier portability, facilitation of specialized and cooperative uses of records, and greater accuracy in their use. Microcopying on motion picture film was compared with photography on glass by Patterson (47) who pointed out the following advantages for film: a cheaper negative material; less room required for apparatus and processing; simpler photographing and processing equipment; and less storage space required for negatives. An exhaustive analysis of microcopying covering its varieties, characteristics, products and costs in comparison to other economical methods of reproducing research materials was presented by Binkley (45).

After outlining the early development of copying of documents on films and mentioning such events as the circularization of American libraries by La Société des Editions sur Films des Bibliothèques Nationales de France, Henry's early articles (23, 26), Library of Congress's Project A which beginning in 1928 copied on film hundreds of thousands of pages of European manuscripts relating to America in European archives, the development of mechanisms for copying and reading bank checks and similar business documents by the Recordak Corporation, Bendikson's early studies (20, 42), and Binkley's pioneer work (16) in appraising microcopy for reproducing research materials. Metcalf (46) surveyed also developments during 1935, mentioning among others the photocopying of 286,000 pages of NRA and AAA hearings, the beginning of microfilming of newspapers both current and back files, the start of the Bibliofilm Service, the activities of Science Service in the field, the arrangement made by Eugene B. Power with the British Museum for the copying of English books before 1550, the services of Photo Copie, GmbH. in Berlin, and tests in progress at the National Bureau of Standards on the permanence of acetate film.

As problems retarding further development, Metcalf mentioned the lack of a central organization to give advice to librarians, individuals and manufacturers, to direct further development, and to arrange for stocks of master negatives from which prints could be made; the need for better cameras and readers; the need for agreement on film width, perforations, orientation of the image, reduction ratios, and the area of film to be viewed at one time. In the same paper he proposed the formation of a non-profit organization with a revolving fund of $25,000 to make a large collection of master film and to make a down payment of $35 on 300 projectors to be distributed to libraries so that the use of film would be facilitated.

Saint Rat (61), writing primarily for French readers, surveyed the history of microcopying, its recent development, and its current state, describing available equipment and including two pictures of the S.R.S. camera. He described a form of slotted card for holding strips of film.

Grant (62), writing for scholars and librarians in a book published in 1937, viewed microcopying as a promising development, but one which was still in the experimental stage. However, he did consider that film slides were well established as a substitute for glass lantern slides. A trip through five European countries was reported by Rush (63), who described the microfilming activities of Kramer at the Staatsbibliothek and at his Photo Copie shop in Berlin where negatives of high quality and 2,000-3,000 enlarged positive paper prints were being made daily; the cameras made by Kontophot; microfilm activities under Schürmeyer at Frankfort, and at The Hague under Duyvis and de Voogd. He mentioned also the work of Loosjes, van Iterson, Page and Sayce; and of commercial firms, particularly La Cinescopie and La Photoscopie.

At the 1936 conference of the American Library Association, a special group of papers presenting basic information on microcopying was read and was later published in book form (64). This was followed up the next year with another group of papers on recent developments. Tate (65) surveyed, primarily for American libraries, the developments in microphotography during the period May 1936-May 1937. He described in a semi-technical manner various cameras, including the Recordak and the Photorecord; mentioned the introduction of Kodak Microfile film, Eastman Fine Grain film, and other developments in film, outlined developments in processing; mentioned the major microfilming projects completed or in progress; and discussed still unfilled needs.

Fussler (66), addressing participants in an international conference held in Europe, described recent microcopying developments in the United States of America, including new equipment, major projects, establishment of the American Documentation Institute, and activities of the American Library Association's Committee on Photographic Reproduction of Materials and of some of the largest libraries. Addressing the same conference, Schüermeyer (67) presented an international survey of photography in documentation, emphasized microcopying and microfilm. He included much information on apparatus.

In a paper addressed primarily to college librarians, Raney (68) gave advice on setting up a microphotographic laboratory or department. He mentioned the basic literature, listed the available equipment, quoted Fussler on the subject of minimum equipment required, and discussed the uses of this equipment.

.Hodgson (69) discussed microcopies from the point of view of librarians and users. He summed up the requirements as he then saw them in the following statement (p. 249):

> 1. Part of the reproduced material must be readable by the naked unaided eye. 2. Most of the material should be reduced from 8 to 20 diameters which would require magnification for reading. 3. Individual pieces for libraries should contain about the same quantity of material as an ordinary book--say 200 to 500 pages. The scholar may need as little as five pages at one time. 4. It should be possible to reproduce varying-sized pages

in the same series. 5. Individual pieces should be easy to store, catalog, find, and use--in other words they should be easy to handle. 6. The actual use of the material by a reader should not be very much different from the use of a full-sized book.

Discussing reductions, Hodgson came to the conclusion that 35 mm. film is too narrow, and that a 40 mm. or 60 mm. film or paper strip would be better. However, he pointed out that even 60 mm. film would have to be rolled, which is inconvenient and subjects the film to wear. Furthermore, such a strip would require photographing and reproducing mechanisms which could work across the film as well as lengthwise of it. He stated that experimentation has shown that 7" x 5" cards are adaptable to the different types of documentary material, then listed these advantages of this form: ease in filing, convenience in handling, ease in insertion in a reading machine. He suggested sheets the size of standard catalog cards for articles of five to ten pages.

In a general survey of microphotography addressed to librarians, Page and Sayce (70) described the advantages, but indicated they did not consider the then current forms and processes final. They viewed spools of film as essentially a reversion to the papyrus roll which had been superseded by the codex more than 2,000 years previously. They predicted that it would soon be possible to print 500 pages or more upon a stiff piece of film the size of a standard index card. Storage was discussed and also durability of film under conditions of library use.

The wide potential applications of microcopying was stressed by Binkley (71) who pointed out that unique copies could be made on demand at costs within the normal price range of books or below it, and that costs are even lower when a large number of copies of the same text is made. There are wide technical differences between the run of a few pages and the run of many thousand, and also between the low reduction ratio of 10 to 12 diameters and the high reduction of 18 to 20 diameters. Cooperative ventures by groups of libraries are discussed, and hypothetical costs of 10 million pages of text shared by ten libraries are cited. Some aspects of the costs of filling individual orders for short runs are considered. Finally, the author made some comments on the use of microfilm for the preservation of documentary material.

A rather detailed analysis of microphotography was presented by Tate (72) who pointed out that the process is distinctly different from motion picture photography. The steps in the microphotographic process are diagrammed in a chart and verbally described. The specialized camera is described. Placement of images on the film is discussed and illustrated in relation to the reductions required. Four kinds of microphotographs are noted: full color, full tone, contrast, and corrected; and the uses of each are discussed.

While recognizing that microfilm will serve the need of some scholars, Bendikson (73) discussed it primarily as the first step in other microcopying processes. Again he pointed out the advantages of low reduction microprints on paper. He recommended that libraries make negative microfilm copies of their rare volumes and documents and preserve these film copies carefully. Only prints made from these master negatives would be issued to scholars. Paper microprints which could be read with a binocular microscope and enlarged photocopies (photostats) requiring no optical aid are discussed. Schürmeyer (74) discussed photocopying primarily for German librarians, comparing film copies to standard photocopies and the latter with enlargements made from film, the durability of acetate film, the storage of films in libraries, the use of microfilm in place of library loans. In passing he described the Union Catalog in Philadelphia as an example of use of microfilm.

The planning, organization and furnishing of a department of microphotography in the library of Temple University was described by Danton (75) who discussed many of the items of equipment in detail as to their uses, special points, etc. List prices of the equipment are given, also a floor plan of the laboratory. A critique of Danton's article by Beveridge (76) and an answer to Beveridge's criticisms by Danton (77) appeared the next year. In his reply Danton added some interesting comments on specific articles of equipment.

Jenkinson and Sayce (78) discussed the use of microphotography in the copying of archival material, pointing out that such copying differs considerably from the copying of books. By using fine grain film with an adequate resolving power, panchromatic emulsions and suitable light filters, archival material can be photographed so that a microcopy on 35 mm. film will show as much detail as the larger negatives used in conventional photography. However, because of the varying sizes of archival material, the varying colors of ink and paper, etc., the position of the camera and the focus must be readjusted frequently and experimental exposures made to determine the best conditions. For these reasons, the speed attained in book copying can never be reached in archival work.

A demonstration of microphotography under the management of the University of Chicago was held at the Paris International Exposition in 1937. A considerable quantity of microcopy was made in full view of visitors. How the demonstration was financed, organized and operated were outlined by Fussler (79), a participant. The Photoduplication Service of the Library of Congress was established March 1, 1938 with the purpose of supplying scholars at a distance with photoduplicates, including microfilms of materials in the Library of Congress (80).

The need in Great Britain for a central microcopying service to operate on a non-profit basis in supplying microfilm copy to institutions and individuals and to assist in the publication and preservation of documentary material was expressed by Page (81). The history and contemporary state of microcopying in France was surveyed by LeRoy (82). Dagron's work is mentioned and there is considerable discussion of the aborted venture of the Société des Editions sur Films des Bibliothèques Nationales de France. The microfilm demonstration at the International Exposition, the S.R.S. camera, Sébille's automatic catalog on film, and the microfilm activities of the Bibliothèque Nationale are all briefly discussed.

A generalized survey of microfilm developments in the United States of America covering history, machines and methods was presented by Raney (83) to an international conference. Power (84), addressing primarily American readers, surveyed the European scene, describing activities, charges, international cooperation, etc. Sayce (85) presented to British librarians a panoramic view of accomplishments and projects in the United States of America with briefer mentions of activities in Great Britain and Europe, discussing such aspects as history, materials, mechanisms, storage and major achievements.

In an article which is primarily a history of the International Federation for Documentation, Duyvis (55) described the activities of this organization in documentary reproduction, including microcopying, and covered also similar activities country by country throughout Europe. Rogers (86), then Director of Research for the New York Herald Tribune, told how he and a co-worker suggested to Eastman Kodak that newspapers could be preserved on film. After a reader had been developed by Eastman, the Herald Tribune microfilmed its own file, reducing the space occupied from 181,571 cu. ft. to 28 cu. ft.

The limitations of microfilm copies from the standpoint of bibliographic study were discussed by Jackson (87), who pointed out that the "feel" of the original book or document is essential in detecting cancels, facsimile leaves and changes of paper in old and rare volumes. Danton (88) published a complementary report on the Microphotographic Department (75) of the library of Temple University, describing the experience since the operation began in October, 1938 and making pointed comments on specific equipment and supplies. Among the processes of technical interest reported on is the making of 35 mm. film positives by copying large scale paper negatives.

Seidell (89) discussed the question of whether a charge should be made by libraries for microfilm copying since charges are not made for services given when readers come in person to the library. The special problems of editing archival records for microcopying were discussed by Edsall (90). The practice of the United States National Archives in making copies on order of microcopies on file is described in the same article.

As a first experiment in the preservation of newspaper files on microfilm, the Library of Congress (91) copied on 125 reels the Washington Post from 1877 to 1904, and the Washington Weekly Post from 1894 to 1900. Microfilming along with other copying processes was discussed from a practical viewpoint by Greenwood (92) in a book which stressed the use of document photography in commerce and industry and described apparatus, techniques and other aspects of the subject.

Mehne (93), addressing a conference on documentation in Germany, compared roll and flat film as material for copying archives for protection in wartime He concluded that flat film was better because of the ease of locating material on it. Rahts (94), addressing the same conference and also talking from the standpoint of preservation of research materials, reviewed microcopying techniques in general and paid particular attention to reduction, suiting the method of copying to the kind of reproduction desired, and storage. The microfilm reading room of the Library of Congress (95) reported that it had 9,045 reels of film.

Microfilming was the subject of an entire book by DeSola (96) who covered history, terminology, uses, advantages, photography, processing, printing, reading and filing, altogether presenting a concise description of the state of the art, with pictures of apparatus and products. Progress in microfilm since 1942 was surveyed by Moholy (97) who discussed standardization with particular reference to British Standard 1153-1944; filing and storing of films; pointed out the need for national and international organization for the lending of microfilms; deplored the lack of suitable readers; and briefly sketched the development of microprint.

Metcalf (98) outlined again the history and development of microfilm, mentioning among other highlights the Recordak Corporation's inquiry of the New York Public Library about possible library uses of microfilm, the Carnegie Corporation's grant to the National Bureau of Standards to underwrite testing of the durability of microfilm, the establishment of microfilm laboratories at Yale University and the University of Chicago, and publication of the Journal of documentary reproduction. He surveyed the library uses of microfilm, described some available equipment and services, and discussed future prospects. He foresaw an increase in the use of microfilm, but doubted if the increase would be as tremendous as some had prophesied. Discussing microcards, he described them as a "grand idea," but predicted that the greatest development in microprinting was likely to be in photo-offset reproductions reduced only two to five diameters.

Moholy (99), then Director of the Aslib Microfilm Service, discussed the contemporary status of microfilm with particular reference to the situation in Great Britain. She listed twelve problems then confronting documentary reproduction, including selection of the most suitable technique, copyright, costs, filing methods, indexing methods, projectors and reading machines. Later in her article she discussed perforated versus unperforated film, film widths, and the most suitable uses for the 16 mm. and 35 mm. widths. She discussed selected developments in the United States of America, particularly Binkley's Manual and the Journal of documentary reproduction, and pointed out the significance to microphotography of the 14th conference of the International Federation of Documentation. Bush (100) published a seminal essay on the scholar's need for documentation and of the potentialities of photography and retrieval mechanisms in filling that need.

The development and post-war state of microfilm was discussed by Saint Rat (101) who gave more attention to sheet microfilm than was customarily paid by contemporary American writers. Tate (102) wrote a brief survey of developments in microcopying during World War II in the United States of America with some references to France, Holland and other European countries. He mentioned equipment developed in the V-mail program, Readex microprint, Rider's Microcards, etc. Moholy (103) gave a detailed account of the Aslib Microfilm Service, which during World War II carried out an extensive program of furnishing microfilm copies of periodicals published in enemy countries. Equipment used is briefly described; organization, financing and methods of operation are discussed; charges are listed; accomplishments are described and tabulated. The same author (104) surveyed the contemporary situation from an international viewpoint and made recommendations for activity in the field on the part of the International Federation for Documentation.

In still another paper Moholy (105) addressed scientists in general and outlined the history of microfilm and some of its achievements, particularly the Aslib Microfilm Service. She pointed out that documentary reproduction is more than a substitute for copying by hand, then listed 20 tasks to which it is adapted, including publication, interlibrary loans, etc. The contemporary state of international cooperation was outlined and a suggestion for organizing it was made. The U.S. War Department (106) published a Technical manual on the uses and limitations of microfilm in the War Department; basic operating procedures for microfilming projects; special techniques which included numbering systems, index card files and special kinds of materials such as engineering drawings and books. This publication included also a guide for operators of microfilm cameras and a guide for inspectors of developed microfilm.

Sheet film rather than roll film was preferred in an analysis by Redepenning (107) of the problems of microcopy, who discussed the advantages and disadvantages of both types, but devoted most of his attention to reading machines. The pros and cons of roll film versus flat film (microfiches) were discussed also by Siedentopf (108) in a general discussion of microcopy addressed to scientists. In addition to form, they commented on reduction ratios, durability of film, methods of making positive sheets and cards from strip film, the need for standardization, and readers.

Downs (109) in a survey of work in progress in the United States of America on documentary reproduction by photography, including microfilm, listed ten active committees and described their work. In the same article he summarized the interest of learned societies, research libraries and commercial firms in this field. Progress in documentary reproduction and especially in microphotography in the period 1936-1946 was outlined by Tate (110). He described some of the uses of microphotography in World War II, major civilian microfilming projects, Microprint, Microcards, and readers. Finally, he pointed out the need on the part of scholars and scientists for more information on documentation and microreproduction.

The president (111) of University Microfilms, Inc. outlined the history of his firm, the first commercial microfilm service for libraries and scholars in the United States of America, then discussed, with concrete examples, six uses of microfilm, namely 1. as a means of protecting books, manuscripts and documents against loss and unnecessary use, 2. securing permanent copies of ephemeral material, 3. obtaining copies of material in distant depositories, 4. reducing the space occupied by a collection of materials in traditional formats, 5. original publication of scholarly and technical material, 6. republishing material in short supply or out of print. Often the examples described were in themselves important steps in the progress of microfilming.

Microfilming was described for museum personnel by Forsdyke (112) who discussed in an introductory and practical manner costs, cameras, projectors, and described the microfilm service of the British Museum. Some of the difficulties encountered in operating the photocopying service of the American Chemical Society and also some of the achievements were described by Emery (113). His paper is addressed to chemists, but is of interest also to documentalists, librarians and managers of photocopying services. Experiences in filling gaps in serial sets with microfilm copies and in making the copies available to readers, most of whom worked from the shelves, are described by Jolley (114), who gave many details of the photographing, storage, and cataloging methods used in an English college library. Fielstra (115) reported on the results of efforts to copy maps on microfilm in order to reduce the space needed for storage, and concluded that microcopying of maps was feasible only for a small proportion of maps in a typical library map collection.

Tate (116) presented at the Symposium on Microdocumentation sponsored by the Division of Chemical Literature of the American Chemical Society, a broad and detailed picture of microfilm, discussing its forms, its potentialities for reduction of copy, how it is made, its uses in recording and preservation of information, its uses in the transport, exchange and publication of information, the commercial microfilm industry, institutional microfilm services, objections to microfilm on the part of users, and the need for fuller use of the techniques of microcopying by scientists and scholars. Power (117) proposed the copying of periodicals on microfilm at a reduction of 20:1 and discussed the economies that would be possible if a group of libraries subscribed to such copies and kept them rather than binding and storing the same periodicals in letterpress format. He discussed more briefly some of the problems of standardization of microcopy. A history of microfilm from 1870 and a description of the equipment displayed at an exhibition of microfilm and photocopy was prepared by Saint Rat (118).

Although they viewed sheet film as superior to film in strips and rolls for documentary microcopying, van der Wolk and Tonnon (119) presented descriptions and critical reviews of the advantages and disadvantages of ribbon film, film strips, Bendikson's and van Iterson's low-reduction microphotographs on paper, Readex Microprint and opaque microcards as advocated by Rider. All of this material was presented as a background to a full discussion of microcopies on sheet film.

The outstanding event in microphotography in 1951 was the publication of the results of an international survey of microphotographic equipment, materials and techniques which was conducted for Unesco (120) by H. R. Verry. The study was designed to prepare the way for international standardization and coordination of documentary microcopying, and both the findings and Verry's recommendations pointed to the need for much work in these areas. Bastardie (213, 214) summarized Verry's findings and tabulated the data on available equipment. Rider (121) discussed the varieties and sizes of microcopy formats and urged the adoption of a single standard size measuring 7-1/2 x 12-1/2 cm. for both opaque and transparent forms. The technique of microfilming in libraries was the subject of a report by Wood (122), submitted to Western Reserve University in partial fulfillment of the requirements for the degree of Master of Science in Library Science. After an outline of the history of the development of microphotography and a brief discussion of selected administrative aspects of microfilm in libraries, this author covered in detail film, cameras, processing equipment, readers, printers and recommended practices and procedures.

A general, informal survey of recent developments in microcopying in Germany together with the author's impression of the use of microfilm in the United States of America was written by Bauhuis (123). Born (124) discussed the policies, activities and potentialities of the Library of Congress in microfilming, but did not cover techniques. A general survey, international in viewpoint, of recent developments was written by Coblans (125), while Spohr (126) surveyed uses and forms of documentary photocopies.

The Federation International de Documentation (127) published a comprehensive description of all methods of documentary reproduction in which microcopying processes are authoritatively discussed in regard to uses, advantages and disadvantages, comparative costs, etc. Addressing South African librarians, Spohr (128) presented an international view of recent developments, and Born (129) described activity in Italy including the publication (and contents) of the first issue of the Bollettino di informazioni sulla microriproduzione.

Microcopies were surveyed from the librarian's point of view by Randall (130) who pointed out advantages of microprint and microcards over microfilm for most library applications. Fussler (131) discussed forms of microcopies from the standpoint of their uses in reproducing research materials. Tate (132) analyzed both transparent and opaque forms from the standpoint of library applications, primarily in the acquisition of materials. His paper includes a convenient chart of uses. The history, activities, equipment and techniques of the Photoduplication Service of the Library of Congress were described by Holmes (133) in an article which is outstanding for explicit descriptions of technical processes.

Born (134) reviewed international differences in methods and terminology and deplored especially the confusion of terms. The Committee on Terminology of the National Microfilm Association (135) sponsored a glossary which was published as a separate (136) under a variant title in 1955. Ballou (137) wrote an authoritative survey of microcopying from the viewpoint of its applications and uses in storing, retrieving and reproducing information.

The Committee on Photoduplication and Multiple Copying Methods of the American Library Association (138) prepared a guide designed to aid microfilm laboratories in standardizing their production of permanent record microfilm. Based largely, but not altogether, on American Standards Association standards, this publication also delineates good procedures in areas not yet covered by American Standards Association standards. The advantages and disadvantages of the more important forms of microcopy were discussed in an article by Webb (139) who pointed out that the microcopying of such colored materials as maps was still unsatisfactory by any method. An integrated system of microfilm copying and reproduction designed for the rapid production of enlarged copies of high quality of maps and other difficult material was exhibited at the Joint Congress of the American Society of Photogrammetry and American Congress of Surveying in March 1955, and was described in an anynymous article (140).

Cain (141), writing from a British viewpoint, surveyed the contemporary uses of microfilm, described several major microfilming projects and listed some official British publications and standards on methods, materials and equipment. The use of microfilm by The New York Times as a form of publication and as a method of preserving files for internal use was described by Lewis (142) who carefully presented the factors in the selection of 35 mm. film for some uses, 70 mm. film for other uses.

All developed techniques of microcopying are covered in an important book by Lewis and Offenhauser (143). Although the main subject in preservation of records in industry and much space is devoted to management and legal questions, library and archival applications, also, are well covered. The use of 70 mm. microfilm as a medium for the preservation of a file of photographs for research purposes was described by Henebry (144). Industrial applications of microcopying were the subject of a book by Herrmann (145), in which microfilm is discussed along with other processes of rapid copying, and of an article by Bobb (146), who discussed procedures in the management and preservation of business records.

Tate (147) in an energetic analysis of available processes for reproduction of documentary materials pointed out the need for basic data and cooperative action in applying to informational documentation the equipment, materials and processes already well developed, largely under the impetus of business and industrial needs. He pointed out that microcopying techniques are distinguished from other reproduction techniques by the fact that the final product requires some kind of reading machine for use and that all such techniques are shown to be based on photography even though the end product may be other than a photographic negative or print.

The current status, material costs, and applicability in library work of the various photographic processes, including microcopying, were the subject of an article by Ballou (148), and this article inspired one by Varden (149) who buttressed several of Ballou's statements but took issue with one of his comments on Xerography. McDonald (150) writing on the disadvantages of microfilm in documentary reproduction, indicated that misleading statements are often made on the economy and space-saving features of microfilm, that such material as drawings are difficult to copy and the filmed copies are often difficult to use; that in general the reading of microfilm is time-consuming. He pointed out that the preparation necessary for microcopying of colored and other difficult material is costly and that editing of the developed film is a laborious job, which is sometimes not done thoroughly. Low cost record storage centers for the preservation of original materials are suggested as a better solution than microfilming.

Stevens (151) authored a book, published in 1957, in which there is a valuable 45-page chapter on document microphotography in addition to useful information on microphotographic techniques in other chapters. This special chapter is a concise presentation in which such aspects as historical development, need for the technique, legal problems, reading and enlargement of microcopies, and future development of document microphotography are discussed. In commenting on the historical development, the author points out that satisfactory materials and equipment were not available, nor was there a pressing demand for document microphotography when the technique was first proposed, but that "...document photography is now a necessity, and activities of great social value would be seriously hampered without its aid..."

Equipment and Materials

Undoubtedly Dagron and other early photographers who experimented with copying documentary material in microform had equipment which could make and reproduce microcopies. Nevertheless, the development of practical devices for document microphotography as we know it today began in the 1930's. One impetus came from the marketing of George I. McCarthy's Checkograph (better known under its later name Recordak), a device for the microcopying of bank checks. Another came from the sporadic use by individual scholars of the Leica and other small cameras in book and manuscript copying for their own purposes.

At least as early as 1930 (152) apparatus described as "new" and consisting of a small camera and projector using motion picture film had been developed by La Cinescopie, a Brussels firm, for manuscript photography and for reading of the film. In the same year Reko (15) addressing scholars, discussed copying from books with the Leica camera. The Leitz focusing screen (153) was a special accessory which facilitated documentary copying with this camera. Henry (23) in a general report on film copies and copying in the large research libraries of America, made several mentions of the equipment then in use without, however, attempting a thorough survey.

Numerous cameras and accessories for microcopying of documents were adapted or invented by individual workers. One constructed by T. Selman, a Swedish architect, is described by Björkbom (154). This camera was mounted on four legs to which lamps were attached for lighting the material to be copied. Focusing was achieved automatically by placing the legs at the corners of the book or other object being photographed. A film of the size 24 x 34 mm. was used. F. G. Ludwig and L. H. Ott, associated with the Sterling Library, Yale University, developed a specialized copying camera (155) using 35 mm. film in 100-foot lengths which came to be known as the Ludwig-Ott camera.

Techniques of using the Contax, another small camera using 35 mm. film for copying from books, were described by

McKay (156). Accessories, particularly a camera stand, a focusing adapter and lights, are also described. A miniature camera especially adapted for the copying of documents was described by Leitz (157). The Recordak, and Newspaper Recordak, both developments of a subsidiary of the Eastman Kodak Corporation and based on the McCarthy Checkograph, were described by Case who discussed also film from the standpoint of its flammability and durability. Cameras and readers shown at an exposition in Washington, D. C. in 1934 are described by Seidell (158) whose paper includes also seven illustrations of the apparatus shown.

The "Rollofot," an apparatus for copying and reproducing documents invented by H. Steinmeyer and Otto Marker, was described by Schürmeyer (159). This device was designed to copy from books and manuscripts as it was rolled over the surface to be copied. Enlarged and reduced images could be made, but apparently high degrees of reduction were not possible. Technical details of the apparatus are described and illustrated.

Metcalf (46) summarized developments in equipment to about the close of 1935 and indicated some of the problems that remain to be solved in camera mechanisms. He discussed also the problem of film widths, pointing out that 16, 35, and 70 mm. film had all been used, and the problems of perforations and of orientation of images on the film. In the same style he discussed reduction ratios and the size of the film area to be viewed at one time. He made no firm recommendations on any of these points, but instead stated what had been done and the problems. Davis (44) listed the mechanisms for microphotographic duplication then being developed by the Documentation Division of Science Service, but gave no technical details.

Inspired by Bendikson's work, van Iterson (53) developed a camera for placing 18 micro-images of documentary material on a photographic plate measuring 13 x 18 cm. His camera and the accessory book holder and magnifier are described and illustrated. A detailed description (160) with illustrations of a modified form of a Leitz enlarger was published. The device was designed to make photographic enlargements from microfilm and also to project from microfilm for reading at a desk or onto a screen to illustrate a lecture. A new form of projection printer, actually a modified form of a Saltzman enlarger but containing a special lens mount and film advance for 35 mm. film, was announced (161). It was designed to make paper prints from microfilm.

Binkley (162) wrote an excellent analysis of requirements for microcopying cameras with emphasis on camera features affecting materials costs. In his famous Manual (45) he listed the cameras then available. Under "Class I, Cameras designed to serve for practical photography, but adapted to use in document copying," appear Cinescopie (Belgium); EKA camera, with Lemare accessories (used by the Library of Congress in copying foreign archives); Leica camera, with Leica accessories; Contax camera, with Zeiss accessories; Argus camera; Bantam Kodak; while under "Class II, Cameras designed primarily for document copying," are listed the Ansco Universal copying camera; Ludwig camera; Filmograph (not on the market as apparatus); Draeger camera; commercial Recordak; Newspaper Recordak; Eastman bound-volume copying camera, 16 mm. film (in process of development); Eastman bound-volume copying camera for newspapers, 35 mm. film; Kennedy camera; Folmer-Graflex photocopying camera (in course of development); and Matson camera (built for Edwards Brothers, Ann Arbor). Fairly detailed descriptions of these cameras, together with illustrations of some of them, are to be found on pages 161-172 of this work, and Table XLVII in it summarizes their chief characteristics, providing information on camera name, manufacturer, price, degree of portability, dimensions of film used, lens, whether the camera will copy bound materials, frame exposure and automatic features.

One of the earliest, specially designed book copying cameras was described technically and its special features discussed by the camera's inventor (163). Photographs of the camera are shown. This camera was designed for using 35 mm. positive motion picture film. Patterson described a special camera convertible into a projector which was made for the Armstrong College Library. A special feature under the title "Microphotography notes," the first issue of which was written by M. L. Raney (49) began publication in the Bulletin of the American Library Association. This column during the course of its existence published numerous news items about new equipment and supplies, not all of which are noted in the present survey.

On page 122 of the Binkley Manual (45) films and emulsions for microcopying are discussed. The author states that the most widely used emulsion at the time was the positive process emulsion used chiefly to make positive prints of motion picture films; but that a panchromatic emulsion is preferable when colored paper or faded inks are to be copied. He states further that the emulsion used by the Recordak Company, although not panchromatic, is more receptive to color contrasts than positive motion picture emulsion. DuPont quarter-speed pan and Eastman micro pan also are recommended for color work. Draeger (164), surveying photographic emulsions and media, devoted most of his attention to motion picture safety film. He forecast that improved emulsions for microcopying would be developed.

Cameras available for microcopying in 1937 were surveyed by Raney (165) who mentioned the Argus, Bantam, Leica, Ludwig-Ott, Micro-Record, the Photorecord, the cameras of R. H. Draeger, the Newspaper Recordak, and the Micro-File Recordak. All are described specifically with prices, sizes of film used and film capacity given for each machine. The mechanics of operating the Recordak machines are described. The camera known as the Seidell-Saint-Rat camera was described by Seidell (166) in one article, and by Saint Rat (167) in another. This camera was designed for stability and simplicity of operation. Its technical features are fully described, and each article contains a photograph of the camera. Accessories for film developing are described also in Seidell's paper.

The Folmer-Graflex Corporation (168) issued an operating manual for its Photorecord camera in which the camera mechanism and the technical details of operating it are described primarily for operators. Draeger (169), addressing an international conference, discussed in a semi-technical style the requirements for microphotography cameras, with special reference to cameras built by him. Addressing American librarians primarily (170), he described the camera which he built for the University of Chicago libraries and which was demonstrated at the Paris Exposition in 1937.

Bendikson (171) discussed work done at the Huntington Library with a Leica camera and at the Armstrong College Library with a Sayce-Watson camera. Both cameras had been used to make relatively low reduction microcopies, positive prints of which on paper could be read with a low-power, wide field binocular microscope. Macalpine (172), commenting upon and supplementing Bendikson's paper, verified that although information on the work at the library of Armstrong College was not published until 1936, the method of photography described was in use there in 1931. Dr. Sayce is quoted to the effect that the limit of reduction is set by the emulsion, and that for positive motion picture film in ordinary processing it is 20 diameters. The Sayce-Watson camera is described by Sayce in quoted remarks as a compromise lacking in automatic features in order to keep its price at a minimum and purposely adapted to the use of short strips of film.

An adequately financed and carefully planned microphotographic laboratory was designed and installed at the University of Chicago. Fussler (173) describes the plan, equipment, even the precautions against dust in the air and suspended matter in the water. A completely mechanized, continuous processing machine then being built for the laboratory and a new camera designed by R. H. Draeger for it are fully described. A considerable range of equipment is covered by Rush (63) in an informal report of a survey of European developments based on a trip through five countries. However, his technical details are sketchy or, in some cases, lacking altogether. He did state that the cameras in use in Berlin "cannot compete favorably with the two large American cameras designed for both speed and capacity."

Tate (65), surveying developments, particularly in the United States of America from May, 1936 to May, 1937, mentions the Recordak cameras for newspaper and bound volume copying and states that with a bound volume machine and a semi-automatic copy holder 750 pages were copied at a reduction ratio of 18 diameters on 35 mm. film in 30 minutes. Two Draeger cameras, the Folmer-Graflex Photorecord, and a Ludwig-Ott all metal camera are described. The introduction of Kodak Microfile Safety Film, Eastman Fine-Grain Safety Film and various emulsions specifically designed for microcopying by the Agfa-Ansco Corporation are mentioned. Developments in processing equipment are outlined in a general way and the processor developed by Holloway is described. It is stated: "To date no positive printer specifically for microfilm has been placed on the market. However, various organizations have made up experimental printers or have adapted motion picture printers."

Microcopying equipment was discussed by Fussler (174) from the viewpoint of smaller libraries. It is pointed out that equipment may range from a simple outfit consisting of an inexpensive camera, a home-rigged copying stand, a cheap developing tank to a specialized camera such as the Photorecord, larger film reels and developing tanks, and suitable printers and enlargers. Contemporary prices are quoted.

In an article published in 1938, Johnson (175) described experiences in photographic copying of documents which were probably typical of the efforts of a number of scholars to adapt photography to note taking. He began document copying about 1905 with a 5" x 7" plate camera. A few years later he conceived the idea of photographing two documents on one plate. The developed plate was used to produce prints enlarged to 6" x 10", or 8" x 10", or was read with a reading glass. In 1908 he purchased a 4.5 x 6 cm. German camera and had it fitted with special plate holders. The plates were read with a strong reading glass or were used to make enlarged prints. In 1910 or 1911 he had an attachment made for this camera which enabled him to load it with about 100 feet of unperforated film on two spools. The picture was about 31 x 49 mm. The exposed film while still in the camera was cut into short strips because of the lack of facilities for developing long lengths. Various improvements which are described were made and at the time the article was written the author had a camera which would take 100 to 120 feet of film and could be loaded in daylight. For manuscript reproduction he found positive film superior to negative film.

The Record Registry camera, a machine developed on the basis of the experience of the Record Registry Corporation, a firm specializing in the photography of public records, was described, with illustrations, by Kerrins (176). Although weighing 98 pounds, this camera was designed to be portable. The Reducagraph camera (177), developed by the National Microfilming Company as part of its scheme for high-reduction microfilm books, was described. This camera weighed 350 pounds, used 35 mm. film, had a copy table capable of holding newspaper size pages down to 3" x 5" index cards, speed was adjustable from 100 to 900 exposures per hour, and exposures could be varied in three ways, lens stop, light control and motor speed. Holbrook (178) described the Holbrook Microfilming camera, a machine using either 16 mm. or 35 mm. film either with or without perforations, and capable of copying a document of any size up to a double-page newspaper spread. A picture of the camera is included in the article.

Completion of the Draeger newspaper copying camera (179) for the Bibliofilm Service was noted. This was a fully automatic camera with a reciprocating carriage designed to position the left-hand page of an open bound volume, then the right-hand page for photographing. Experience with the Photorecord camera in the National Park Service was described by Stauffer (180) who reported that the pneumatic foot release was "not altogether foolproof" and that the camera arm had a tendency to move slightly during copying. Raney (181) discussed the automatic features that were sought in equipment for the American demonstration of microcopying at the Paris Exposition in 1937. From this standpoint he discussed the Draeger and Photorecord cameras and an automatic processor built by the Holloway Company.

Cameras and related equipment available in 1938 are described at length in an important survey sponsored by the Journal of documentary reproduction (182). The characteristics of 22 cameras used in microphotography, including such information as manufacturer, country where built, number built, size of film used, capacity, operating speed, and "results in expert hands" are given. The cameras are classed as 1. adapted, 2. small special cameras designed for microphotography, and high speed production cameras. Group features and features of individual cameras falling within the groups are described, and several cameras then under development are mentioned.

Equipment available in the U.S.A. for making projection prints, including enlargements, together with some machines still under development, was concisely described. Enlargers offered by Eastman Kodak, Folmer Graflex, Leitz, International Research, and J. G. Saltzmann were mentioned. A microfilm unit offered by the Photostat Corporation for adapting Photostat machines for printing microfilm enlargements on Photostat paper is described.

The same article includes a survey of emulsions and bases, including not only standard film but also Ozaphane and paper. Emulsions are classified as follows: 1. color blind or non-color sensitive, 2. orthochromatic or partially color sensitive, 3. panchromatic or fully color sensitive, and 4. special emulsions. The problems of grain size is discussed and specific films including Eastman Microfile and Agfa Document are mentioned. Ozaphane film is discussed at some length and problems in emulsions and bases still requiring research are mentioned. The processing of film is outlined in some detail with a distinction made between film intended for ordinary use and film intended for permanent records. The processing of paper is not covered. Needed equipment is mentioned.

Haughton (183) listed three basic kinds of microcopying cameras: those used by amateurs and individual researchers; standard, general purpose, microfilm cameras capable of copying a range of document sizes; special purpose cameras designed to copy a single class of document, and gave the names of then active American manufacturers and suppliers of microfilm camera equipment. In an article written to point out the distinguishing features of microphotography as a photographic technique, Tate (72) described the microphotographic camera as a highly specialized instrument with such features as a proportional film advancing mechanism. In the same article, he discussed film for microcopying, mentioning the various widths used, the presence or lack of perforations, variable frame sizes, and the several image placements.

The kinds and makes of film then in use in microphotography were the subject of a short article (184). It is stated that positive motion picture safety film was the type most generally used for both negatives and positives because of such features as fine grain, high contrast and low cost. Eastman's Microfile and Fine-Grain Print films are described, the first as a very fine grain color-sensitive film suitable for negatives, the second as a slow, high contrast film for positives. Developmental work in progress on other films is mentioned. News items pertaining to new equipment introduced by manufacturers were published under the heading "Technical and News Notes" (185) in various issues of the Journal of documentary reproduction. A projection printer put into use by University Microfilms was described (186). This machine was designed to make enlargements on Photostat paper from microfilm negatives at an operating rate of about one frame per second. Prints were delivered in a continuous roll unless the purchaser paid an extra charge for trimming and collating.

The mechanization of microphotographic equipment for the making of microfilm on a fairly large scale was the subject of an article by Fussler (187). Mechanized equipment already constructed and automatic features needed in cameras, processors, printers and enlargers are discussed. The article is concerned with needs and problems rather than the technical details of mechanisms. Cameras were covered along with other topics in a general survey by Sayce (85) of the state of microfilm in 1939. The historical development of special cameras for microcopying was sketched by Raney

(188) who then discussed the Photorecord in more detail, mentioning its features, faults, price and the prices of accessories. Flemer (189) described the Saint-Rat-Seidell camera and compared it with Draeger and Eastman microcopying cameras.

News of camera developments appeared frequently in Fussler's column in the Library journal. One notice (190) described the features of a revised version of the Recordak Micro-File camera, including a fully mechanized book cradle on one model, automatic focusing, rotating camera head and continuously variable film advance. Another notice (191) described changes made in the Photorecord camera, including a new lens, new shutter, new focusing mechanism, and mechanical changes in the magazine. Experimental equipment constructed by Holbrook Microfilms, Inc. for the Photoduplication Service of the Library of Congress is described in another issue of the same column (192). One piece of apparatus was a camera specifically designed for the copying of 3" x 5" cards onto 16 mm. film, and a complementary piece was an automatic enlarger designed to print from the 16 mm. film 3" x 5" enlargements on paper at a rapid rate.

Film and photographic emulsions were discussed by Raney (188) from the point of view of microphotography. Printing and enlarging from microfilm also were discussed, and the author deplored the lack of a satisfactory, continuous contact printer for unperforated film. He pointed out also needed improvements in automatic enlargers. With reference to negative film and color film, newly introduced by Agfa for use in microphotography, Rahts (193) discussed the characteristics of microfilm, particularly grain, resolving power, methods of preventing halation, and uniformity.

The whole range of microphotographic equipment installed in a new department of microphotography in a university library is covered by Danton (75). Items of equipment are listed and described individually, the special points of each one are discussed, and list prices are given. Complementary articles by Danton (77, 88) and Beveridge (76) contain further valuable information on specific articles of equipment.

The history of the development of Recordak microfilming and reading apparatus was recounted by Boeing (194), who described in detail the then current models of Recordak, namely Model C1, a semi-automatic machine designed for the photographing of all types of bound and unbound material;

Model C2, designed for photographing large maps, blueprints, drawings and tracings; and Model D, designed for photographing bound and unbound records. Recordak Junior, a combined camera and reader designed for the copying and reading of small quantities of materials is also described along with several models of readers. A microfilm printer specially built for the University of Chicago Libraries and designed to handle 35 mm. nonperforate, single perforate, and double perforate film was described by Fussler (195). The machine had features not then available in commercial equipment which were important in high resolution reproduction.

The use of a Rolleicord II camera with a special 35 mm. back in microcopying was discussed by Worth (196), who described the camera and the adapter back, the necessary supplementary lenses and made comparisons with other hand cameras sometimes used in microcopying. Reid (197) described techniques of making microfilm copies of short runs, such as journal articles, with a small portable camera, the Argus Model C. The characteristics of the camera, a method of supporting it on a laboratory ring stand and the technique of operation are described in detail, primarily for scientists. Cameras and related apparatus designed by Saint Rat, Keegstra and others are mentioned by Duyvis (55), who discussed also developments in sensitive materials, especially the possibility of replacing silver bromide materials with azo and diazo compounds. Technical details, dimensions and a picture of the Recordak Microfilm Enlarger designed for printing on paper from microfilm in enlargements from 8 to 30.5 diameters were supplied in an article by Tate (198).

Laboratory equipment is fully covered in Chapter IX of Fussler's Photographic reproduction for libraries (199). Commercially available apparatus is described and some of it is illustrated. Cameras are divided into adapted machines and those especially designed for microphotography, with the latter group further classified into those commercially produced in quantity and those built in limited numbers by hand. The discussion is limited to the first subgroup. Cameras designed for special types of copying such as accounting are mentioned, but not fully described. The primary attention is given to such equipment as the Photorecord and the Kodak. The technical features, methods of use, and accessories, such as book cradles, are described for cameras of this class.

Commercially available film processing equipment is described in detail in essentially the same way as copying equipment. The Recordak Enlarger, Model A, is fully described and differences in construction between it and the Recordak Precision Enlarger are pointed out. Other enlargers which could be adapted to enlarging from microfilm also were described. It was pointed out that there are two types of positive printers, step and continuous, but that the most prevalent type in microfilm work is the one in which the raw positive film and the negative are advanced continuously past a narrow slip while in contact. A variety of miscellaneous equipment such as voltmeters, ammeters, and light filters were described in the same chapter.

Equipment for microcopying was described in a book on document photography in commerce and industry by Greenwood (92) and in another book by De Sola (96). In both books information on commercially available equipment was presented as a part of the general picture of microcopying and was accompanied by information on other facets of this subject. Equipment used by University Microfilms, Inc. when this firm was first established in 1938 and the improved equipment acquired in subsequent years was described by Power (111). Cameras, processing equipment, printers and miscellaneous equipment such as rewinds were mentioned and their uses indicated. Equipment and supplies used in microfilming operations in the United States War Department were explicitly described in a department Technical manual (105).

Equipment, specifically a Recordak microfilm enlarger and a specially built paper rewind was acquired by the Library of Congress to enable its Photoduplication Service make microfilm enlargements up to 12 inches in width on continuous rolls of paper (200, p. 121). In 1947 the Library of Congress (201, p. 35) acquired an automatic microfilm enlarger which was developed for its Photoduplication Service. It enlarged automatically on a continuous roll of card stock from microfilm. The companion camera copied cards on microfilm at the rate of 360 per minute.

Van Alphen and Dippel (202) discussed the new possibilities opened up by Philips M. D. film, a film originally developed for sound moving pictures in which the sound track is on the margin of the film. This film has an exceptionally high resolving power (1,000 lines per millimeter), and other properties which make it attractive for prints and enlargements for microfilm negatives. The authors compare it for resolution with Kodak Verichrome, Kodak Microfile, and other films used in microcopying. The question of whether available optical instruments are capable of reproducing the minute pictures which theoretically could be made is discussed.

Dippel and Kenning (203), discussing the same film, gave more technical details. They described the chemical reaction which was based on the exposure of a diazonium compound combined with a mercury salt to light. The light causes the mercury to separate in the form of atomic metal. A physical development (in contrast to the chemical development of the silver halides) causes metallic silver to be deposited in the exposed parts of the image. Thus the developed image is composed of silver as in silver halide photography although the basic chemistry of the process is much different. Their article is primarily a discussion of drawbacks in silver halide film, but they discuss also the features of the new film such as high resolving power, locally variable gamma, and lack of grain which are advantageous in microcopying. In still another article, Alink and others (204) described the basic chemistry of the new film, its properties, low cost, etc. Also, they devoted fully a page of their paper to the advantages of the material for microdocumentation.

Philips M. D. film was the starting point for a paper by Oosterloo (205) in which the space-saving potentialities of high reduction microcopies in sheet film are discussed in some detail with most of the argument based on the potentialities of films with less spectacular resolving power.

Taubes (206) wrote a detailed description of the Fassel Photo-File camera, a flow camera which simultaneously photographs the front and back of a sheet being copied in such a way that images appear side by side across the width of the film. A wiring diagram, details of mechanisms and pictures of the camera are included in the paper. Bobb (207) mentioned a microfilm enlarger that was designed to enlarge from 16 mm. to 35 mm. or 70 mm. microfilm upon rolls of sensitized paper at the approximate rate of 750 8" x 10" enlargements per hour. The exposed paper was then processed automatically by a specially constructed continuous processor.

The use of the Leica camera and its appropriate accessories in documentation and other library copying was discussed at length by Schürmeyer (208). Taube (209) described without giving many technical details a Philips camera designed for taking pictures successively across a strip of film of any width and arranged so that the film is automatically advanced at the end of each row of images; in other words, a camera suited to copying on sheets and cards of film rather than reels. Van Santen (210) described a special device which he called "reproductieschuif" or in English, reproduction-slide, whose purpose it was to make an enlarger serve as a microcopying camera. Instructions for building the device were included. Anderson (211) described a Swedish portable microfilm camera which used 35 mm. film and which was designed so that small extracts, for example, a single line of print or a small figure, could be photographed when desired.

Van der Wolk and Tonnon (119) described G. Cordonnier's Polydoc camera, Goebel's microcamera and title camera, Van Iterson's and Kabitz's cameras, all of which are designed primarily for the production of microfiches (transparent sheet film). Comparing the technique of photographing on ribbon film with that of photographing on sheet film or transparent microcards, they point out that the same reduction scale can be used for all of the photos on a sheet of film. In other words, it is not necessary to change the position of the image or the scale of reduction in order to accommodate a larger than usual picture. On the other hand, when a mistake is made in photographing on sheet film, the whole film must be done over. Also, more care is required in photographing on sheet film than on ribbon film because the images are taken in rows. Verry (212) in a summary of the first part of his "Survey of microfilm use" for Unesco described recent developments in European equipment, mentioning in particular Cordonnier's camera which used film on rolls to produce microsheets and Goebel's camera which used cut sheet film. He mentioned also the Debrie automatic processing tank which is described as falling between manual tanks and large automatic machines.

Bastardie (213, 214) prepared a summary of the findings on equipment made in the course of the Unesco (120) international survey of microphotography. Data on microfilm and microfiche cameras commercially available in the various nations in 1951 are presented in a nine-page table. Given are name and address of manufacturer, type of camera, dimension of film used, reduction ratio, size of image, lens, price in the country of manufacture and special points such as automatic focusing, book holders, and provision for variable exposure. The same author in a second supplement (214) summarized the processing of microfilm, that is to say, development, printing and enlargement, and presented in the same style as the table on cameras, data on developing, printing, and enlarging equipment.

Janicki (215) described and included illustrations of machines for microcopying and reading manufactured by three Swiss firms: Optik, A. G., Chur, and Alos, A. G. A German machine for microcopying, the "Microstat," is described in an article by Reichalt (216) along with information on a reader and case for the storage of film. The Microstat appears to have been developed primarily for use by commercial firms.

In an unpublished report, Wood (122) presented in chart form data on the following brands of film: Eastman Microfile, Eastman Positive Safety, Eastman High Contrast positive, DuPont Safety Microcopy, DuPont Safety positive, and DuPont Fine Grain Safety positive. The chart covers trade names, manufacturers' names, methods of packaging, prices as of February, 1951, style of perforation, type of copy work for which suited, resolving lines per millimeter, in addition to processing information.

Included in the same report is a chart of data on 35 mm. microfilm in cameras. These cameras are listed: Recordak Microfile Model C-1, Recordak Microfile D, Recordak Microfile Model E, Folmer Graflex Photorecord, Diebold Flofilm Model 90-46, and Diebold Flofilm Model 90-03. The following points are covered for each camera: manufacturer's name, price as of February, 1951, style, i.e., whether flat bed or rotary, whether for use with flat or bound material, whether for use with perforated or nonperforated film, maximum size of material copied, reduction ratios, lens, focal length, diaphragm setting, exposure times, frame aperture, head rotation, kind of power required for operating; type of focusing, illumination and illumination control, adjustable film advance, warning systems whether portable or stationary, and special features such as built-in exposure meter.

In the same style, Wood covered processing equipment for 35 mm. microfilm. For the Morse G-30, Morse G-10, Microrecord, Fairchild-Smith F-214, Stineman, Nikor, and Diebold, he gave information on the following points: manufacturer's name, price, operating power, film capacity, amount of solution required in processing tank, electric current required, if any, material of construction, whether daylight operation was possible, style (whether portable or stationary), processes accomplished, required lengths of leaders and trailers, processing time, number of tanks, and special features.

Another chart in the Wood report covered the Stineman, Burke and James, Depue and Diebold Camera-Printer Model 90-46, providing information on the following points for each: manufacturer's name, price, operating power, i.e., whether manual or electric, type of film handled, i.e., perforated or unperforated film-moving mechanism, capacity of positive film magazine, printing speed in feet per minute, source of illumination, and illumination control.

In an article dealing with microfilm as a medium for preservation of documents, Offenhauser (217) described such characteristics as the thickness of the emulsion, the thickness of the base, the composition of the emulsion and its "grain." He described the characteristics of the Lippman emulsion which is the finest grained emulsion known, discussed effect of emulsions clumping during development, and the effects of developers.

Microfilm apparatus shown at the International Photographic and Cinematographic Exposition at Cologne and the German Industries Fair at Hanover in 1952 was described by Knigge (218) from the viewpoint of its usefulness in documentation and particularly microfilm copying and reading. Most of the machines described were of contemporary European manufacture. The Library of Congress (219, p. 103) added to the equipment of its Photoduplication Service a Flofilm Duplex Microfilm Camera Model 90-03, and an NDR Microcamera. The first machine was capable of photographing both sides of documents and operating at high speeds. The second machine was an import from the Netherlands and it was designed to produce flat film, for example, cards containing 50 micro-images. It is mentioned that studies were started toward making this camera an automatic one.

The principles and common technical details of microcopying apparatus are summarized in the F.I.D. Manual (127, p. 222.3 E4-5). The summary includes in addition to routine information such helpful points as the need for a warning device to signal when the sensitive material in the camera is used up. Enlarging apparatus is discussed on p. 222.7 E/F1 of the same Manual, where information is given not only on specially built machines and desirable features, but it is also pointed out that some readers and some cameras may be used as enlargers.

The properties of high quality film for microcopying are discussed by Welp (220) who pointed out that speed is essential for rapid copying, high contrast is necessary, but much contrast is undesirable. Good microfilms will have fine grain, thin emulsions and a steep gradation curve. Developing time should be adjusted to the thickness of the emulsion. Newly introduced German materials for documentary reproduction, including Agepe-Halftone paper designed for the reproduction of halftones in microfilm printing and enlargement, were described by Hornung (221).

A simple microcopying apparatus based on a Zeiss-Ikon camera with a 5 cm. lens, an inexpensive accessory lens, which was constructed at the Library of the Royal Faculty of Physicians and Surgeons of Glasgow, was described and illustrated by Gibson and Goodall (222). Reed (223) described a simple copy stand, giving details and illustrations, which is well suited to microcopying by small institutions. The Photoduplication Service of the Library of Congress (224) installed a 70 mm. microfilm camera which had been built to its specifications for the microcopying of charts, drawings and blueprints which could not be satisfactorily reproduced by 35 mm. cameras.

Léauté (224a) discussed from the standpoint of standardization the characteristics of safety film base for microcopies and the requirements for its preservation and storage. A report by Guillot (224b) contained illustrations and specifications of cameras, enlargers, and other microcopying equipment available from French manufacturers in 1955.

An integrated system of specialized equipment designed for the microcopying and full-size reproduction of maps and other finely detailed material was described (140). The system included an automatic processor which used only a small quantity of solution and which also dried the developed film. This machine which was designed to process discontinuous lengths of 16, 35, and 70 mm. film, both black-and-white and color, the processing to be controlled by coded disks, is described in more detail by Peckinpaugh (225).

A broad and detailed survey of microphotographic equipment was presented in a book by Lewis and Offenhauser (143). The chapter on cameras is 50 pages long and covers such aspects as lens performance, including resolving power and camera spools. In addition, it describes in detail selected commercial equipment and gives condensed information on practically all available equipment. The condensed information is presented in a table entitled "Microfilm and Microfilm Cameras" under columns headed "Type," "Price," "Film Size," Reduction Ratio," "Image Size," "Lens Capacity," "Remarks." Cameras currently manufactured in the United States of America, West Germany, East Germany, France, Japan, Great Britain, The Netherlands and Sweden are listed. Processing and enlarging equipment was described along with discussions of techniques in Chapter VII, p. 181-234. Tables of detailed data on processing and enlarging equipment appear on p. 190-193, 195-197, 202-204, and 216-219. These tables cover both equipment manufactured in the United States of America and in certain foreign countries, including France, West Germany and Italy.

Film for microcopying was described by Lewis and Offenhauser in their chapter "The Microrecording Process." General film characteristics such as composition of the base, physical properties of the gelatin and emulsion, and the role played by sensitizing dyes; sensitometric characteristics of film; the three basic types of film, negative, reversal and positive; resolving power or detail rendering, and methods of measuring this property are all discussed in some detail with literature references.

Kiersky (226), in a series of articles in Special libraries, published information on a variety of new developments in equipment, including machines and supplies exhibited at the National Business Show in 1956. A portable microfilming camera which photographs both sides of a document simultaneously and an inexpensive automatic processor which makes enlarged prints from microfilm rolls are among the equipment mentioned in this continuing series of articles. Also described is the Flemer-Seidell microfilm camera, a low-cost machine designed for microfilm copying on a moderate scale. It was equipped with an electrically operated camera capable of 20 exposures per minute. The same device was designed in full technical detail by Flemer and Seidell (227), its developers, in another article. Stevens (151) included (p. 261-265) in his book a condensed presentation of basic camera mechanisms, cameras, and accessories, such as foot controls, used in microcopying. On p. 268-269 he briefly described Cordonnier's Polydoc, the Kabitz, and Goebel cameras for microcopying on sheet film.

Equipment, especially cameras, affects the quality of micro-images. For this reason there is some discussion of equipment in later sections of this report. As a general rule, descriptions of equipment for micrôcopying have been summarized in the preceding paragraphs when there was no special emphasis on quality or production costs, but writings on equipment in which quality of the produced images or production costs were emphasized have been included in the sections entitled Quality Factors and Production Costs.

Photographic Methods

The photographic methods used in microcopying are not basically different in principle from those used in other areas of photography. For this reason, general treatises on photographic theory and handbooks of photographic methods both contain much information of value in microphotography. However, no attempt will be made in this survey to cover general photographic literature. Some of the early works (4, 5, 6, 7) which contain descriptions of techniques of making microscopic images of large objects, including documents, have already been listed because of their historical associations. In this section only material on photographic methods directly presented from the standpoint of microcopying of documentary material will be mentioned. Xerography and diazo type processes are included in subsections under Retrieval and Enlargement because their primary use in microcopying is in the making of enlargements. Since photographic methods are a major factor in the quality of micro-images, much of the writing on quality factors summarized later in this report bears on photographic methods.

The film processor built by Holloway for the University of Chicago libraries and demonstrated at the Paris Exposition in 1937 was described by Holloway (228). A microfilm printer (229) built by G. J. Padgley to exacting specifications drawn up by the American Documentation Institute was briefly described. Among the requirements were perfect safety for the negative, an unblurred image, and a speed of 1,500 exposures per hour. Other technical details of the machine are given.

Processing techniques for microfilm (but not paper or Ozaphane) are described explicitly in "The present status of equipment and supplies for microphotography" (183). The following procedure is recommended for microfilms intended for permanent records: "1. Develop. 2. Rinse (water or acid-rinse bath). 3. Fix. 4. Wash (in ordinary water). 5. Re-fix in fresh fixing bath with or without hardener. 6. Wash for 15 minutes in ordinary water. 7. Wash for 15-30 minutes in distilled water. 8. Test residual "hypo" content; result must be negative. 9. Dry under controlled conditions." Processing techniques for both short and long lengths of film are described in some detail.

The mechanical and photographic problems presented by a collection of archives when it is desired to copy them by microphotography were discussed by Jenkinson and Sayce (230). They treated the subject more from the viewpoint of the archivist than from that of a professional photographer, but included many points of value to a photographer faced with a job of copying archives on microfilm. Saint Rat (231) wrote a technical discussion on the use of ultraviolet light in microcopying such material as faded and overwritten manuscripts, basing it in large part on his own researches but including references to the work of others.

Fussler (232) discussed the use of light filters in relation to types of film and pointed out that filters are of little use with color blind films, such as motion picture positive film, and are usually not necessary in microcopying even when panchromatic film is used. The color sensitive characteristics of the three principal types of emulsions--color blind, orthochromatic and panchromatic--are described from this viewpoint, and the author points out that light filters are necessary in microcopying only under unusual conditions. Danton and Elfont (88) in a description of experience in the photographic laboratory of Temple University included some unusual information on the functioning of copying equipment and described photographic techniques from a practical viewpoint.

The special problems of exposure in document copying were discussed primarily for users of portable cameras by Noll (233). He gave attention to such matters as difference between rated lens aperture and effective aperture, the narrow latitude of document film, and the variations in intensity of light reflected from pages with different ratios of text and background. He covered also developing techniques in some detail.

Crabtree and others (234) discussed the elimination of hypo from photographic images. Although they addressed photographers in general and were not primarily concerned with microimages, their paper is mentioned here because of the importance of hypo elimination from permanent record microfilm and micropaper. They reviewed the history of hypo eliminators, presenting a chronological list, and stated that the majority have not been satisfactory. They proposed a new eliminator consisting of hydrogen peroxide and ammonia, and described in considerable detail the results of their experiments. They mentioned in passing several valuable points pertaining to the effects of hypo photographic images on film and on paper, and made specific recommendations for two treatments, one of which will completely eliminate hypo from prints and the other of which will leave a residue of 0.01 mg. per square inch. Their paper is primarily concerned with elimination of hypo from paper prints, but some information pertinent to hypo elimination in negative processing is included also.

In a paper on the general use of microfilm in the Library of the American Philosophical Society, Garver (235) included information on techniques of checking resolution, density, etc. in the course of making and developing microfilm. In a paper on microphotography written primarily from the photographer's point of view, Stevens (236) discussed the production of microscopic photographs. He stated that therefore such photographs have been made on sensitive materials coated by individual experimenters, but that a commercial dry plate had been made available. He discussed, therefore, the construction and operation of the necessary apparatus and gave special attention to the focusing of minute images. Techniques of film processing in microfilm laboratories were described in detail by Fussler (199) in relation to commercially available processing equipment. Developing, drying, contact printing, and enlarging are all covered. Metcalf (98) discussed microfilm, Readex Microprint, and microcards from the viewpoint of their implications for libraries in the postwar period, including a few technical details, but devoting most of his attention to the future prospects of each form.

A Technical manual published by the United States War Department (106) included specific descriptions of photographic procedures to be followed in microfilming War Department records. Covered were the preparation of records for microcopying with a rotary camera, the operation of rotary microfilm cameras, inspection of developed film, procedures for retakes and splicing. Special techniques such as the copying of engineering drawings and the microfilming of books also were described.

Addressing photographers generally, Tritton (237) described development techniques which adapt microcopying film such as Kodak Microfile to the microcopying of photographs and half-tone reproductions. Special points to be observed in copying such documents as finely detailed drawings and large maps on microfilm were discussed by Boon (238). Ashworth (239) made practical recommendations for developing, fixing and drying of microfilm and included some formulae for processing solutions.

Photographic methods were the primary subject of an unpublished report by Wood (122). In a chart on films in this work, data pertaining to processing for six makes of film are given under the headings: resolving power, meter setting for line work, recommended exposure for negatives under specified illumination, developer and developing time, fixer and fixing time, and type of safe light required. In another chart techniques in production of microfilm are described step by step. Specific practices and procedures are recommended for each step, and alternative or controversial methods also are given for many of them. Each step is specifically described, for example, (p. 56): "Preparing the film for drying. Place in fresh water and swab with soft cotton while under the water. Remove excess water with a clean, damp photo chamois while winding the film onto the drying rack."

A concise statement of microfilm processing after photographing is included in Bastardie's summary (214) of processing equipment. Developing, printing and enlarging techniques are surveyed from the viewpoint of librarians and archivists rather than photographers. Useful information on techniques is presented, such as "the light must be carefully controlled according to the film's density," but specific techniques of operating equipment are not covered. In contrast, specific directions on techniques in making microcopy on microfilm are included in the F.I.D. Manual (127), except on points where the procedures are the same as in ordinary photography. In an article devoted largely to reflex copying, Weigert (240) gave some attention to techniques of microcopying. He described among other things a practical method for using ordinary room light and Plus X film with

Leica equipment and giving one-half second exposure in copying from books.

Although they did not devote a chapter of their book specifically to photographic techniques, Lewis and Offenhauser (143) included much information on this subject with their discussions of films, cameras, enlargers, processors, etc., and with their generalized discussions of processes. Their chapter on cameras, for example, contains approximately six pages on factors affecting image quality and much of the discussion pertains to photographic techniques. Another such passage deals with the importance of good drying of film in processing.

Photographic techniques are a principal subject in a book by Stevens (151). This author discussed for photographers and other readers with a knowledge of photographic terminology the principles and techniques of microphotography. His chapter on technical problems runs from p. 247 to 255 of the volume and contains expert discussions of such matters as exposure. In discussing exposure he emphasized the necessity of an exposure level which will keep the images of the lines "open," which is less than the exposure which would give the highest contrast. A graph representing the relationship between quality of image and density is included. He said further: "...the best average quality is obtained by exposing Microfile film to give background densities in the range 1.2-1.5 (above base); although the emulsion is able to give much higher densities." Some of his material on exposure in relation to quality was drawn from Rudd.

Other points of technique related to recording the image which are discussed include control of brightness of illumination, prevention of "creep" of the copy during exposure, and immediate rephotographing of exposures known to be spoiled. In his discussion of processing, Stevens pointed out that the handling of long lengths of film is the main problem and suggested that whenever possible processing should be done by commercial firms which have equipment for continuous processing in which the image quality is controlled sensitometrically. However, he described conventional processing with Stineman and Nikor spiral reels.

Types and Characteristics

General. Early discussions of the characteristics of

microfilm as a medium for documentary reproduction and publication are to be found in writings by Binkley in 1931 (16) and in 1934 (24). In both publications the author was primarily concerned with comparisons among methods of reproducing research materials, but he gave a good account of the nature and advantages and disadvantages of microfilm. In an article (33) addressed to the scholarly world in general, he compared in less technical terms offset printing, near print methods, and microfilm, pointing out their potentialities and implications for scholars.

Seidell (241) described filmstats (his proposed term for copies of documentary material on strips of film) as a new means for the advancement of science, covering such points as developments to the date of writing, methods and equipment, reductions, and methods of reading. Umbreit (242) compared reproductions on paper and on film and delineated the areas of application of each as he saw them. He analyzed in general terms such factors as costs and degree of technical skill required in making film copies as compared to paper. He estimated microfilm as superior to paper for library and archival use, but pointed out the need for better film reading machines.

In his 1936 Manual (45) Binkley described fully all of the developed microforms applicable to documentary copying and publishing, including not only microfilm but also microprint in the forms developed by Admiral Fiske for reading in his Fiskoscope, by Professor Peters for the publication of theses, and by Bendikson. Examples of these forms were included as laid-in inserts or as text illustrations.

Hodgson (69), analyzing microcopying in general, discussed both film and paper mentioning in his discussion of both media 40 mm. and 60 mm. (!) widths. He was primarily concerned with the degree of reduction required and convenience in using the microcopy. After discussing the disadvantages of strips, primarily on the score of inconvenience, he pointed out the advantages of 7 x 5 inch sheets for copies of some length and 3 x 5 inch cards for short articles. Page and Sayce (70) compared microcopies on film in ribbon form and the same upon stiff film "the size of an ordinary index card," and strongly advocated the latter format saying that the film on spools is a reversion to library methods discarded 2,000 years ago when the papyrus roll was superseded by the codex.

Bendikson (73), advocating the inexpensive contact prints made from microfilm on paper, which he had developed, discussed the advantages and disadvantages, primarily in regard to cost and space, of both film and paper in strip form for use by scholars, while recognizing that both as a first step and for record purposes a microfilm negative is essential. Raney (243) in appraising the status of microphotography also compared film and paper, pointing out that paper costs one-quarter as much as film, but that film could be read by projection while paper microcopies required the use of a magnifying glass. Bendikson's miniature prints on paper are described, and it is mentioned that the Folmer-Graflex Company planned to equip its Photorecord camera with magazines for 70 mm. paper as well as for 35 mm. film, thus making possible direct microcopying on paper.

Metcalf (98) discussed microfilm, Readex microprint and microcards from the viewpoint of their implications for libraries in the postwar period, including a few technical details, but devoting most of his attention to the future prospects of each form. He forecast that "the greatest development in microprinting is more likely to be with photo-offset reproductions reduced by 2 to 5 diameters..."

Redepenning (107) in an analysis of microfilm technique, discussed the characteristics of microfilm and compared roll film and sheet film, pointing out that roll film requires 25 per cent more storage space, is more difficult to use because of the difficulty of locating a needed page, and is easily scratched in rolling. Essentially the disadvantages were listed by Siedentopf (108) who, however, pointed out that roll film was more convenient for copying documents of varying lengths since the length of the film strip could be adjusted as needed.

The Scientific Information Conference sponsored by the Royal Society (244) appointed a working party with the purpose (p. 272) "to compare the technical and economic merits and proper fields of application of microfilm reels, microcards and ultra-microprints," and this party presented a paper in which all of these forms were described and critically examined. The principal fault found with microfilm was the necessity of searching out non-continuous frames, particularly when looking up cross references. It was pointed out also that time was lost in changing from one reel to another and that items on long lengths of film cannot be arranged and classified in alphabetical order nor can new items be interpolated. No such fault was found with microstrips which, it was pointed out, could be stored flat in paper pockets "with tags attached to the ends of strips for indexing purposes." It was stated that there are several forms of microcards, including the rectangular sheets of film known as "microplaque" in France and the opaque form advocated by Rider. The working party noted that both forms are printed from photographically produced masters, but a more flexible process would result if microreproduction could be freed both from 35 mm. film and from printing so that either opaque or transparent microcards could be made by direct photography from the original documents.

In a rejoinder to the working party's report, Forsdyke (244) contributed (p. 702-704) a paper entitled "Relative advantages of microfilm in different forms." He disclaimed being an advocate of continuous film, but believed "unduly hard things" had been said about microfilm rolls. He pointed out that the difficulty of finding a wanted frame on a long strips could be helped by inserting a pilot number every fiftieth page when the film was made; and that frames can be interpolated in a continuous film by splicing. Further, it is easy to duplicate long runs of continuous film in an automatic printer, an advantage which is lost when a film is cut into short strips. Continuous film is better protected and the blank leaders at each end provide a means of safe handling which is lacking in short strips. In contrast, microstrips are not suitable for public libraries or large repositories of records. They require more care in handling and are not so easy to store. The working party found no place in scientific information services for "ultra-microprints," that is, microcopies of extreme reductions.

Power (177), advocating the use of microfilms at a reduction ratio of 20 to 1 for the preservation of journals, compared such microfilms with microcards and emphasized the superior image obtainable from microfilm in readers and projectors. In the same article he mentioned that Europeans prefer strip film to roll film. Tauber (245) summarized the results of a survey of librarians and individuals interested in microdocumentation developments and problems in the use of microfilms, microprint and microcards. Among the complaints were slowness in getting microfilm copies from other libraries, high prices, errors in orders, poor quality of work. Microcards were compared to microfilms for the preservation of newspapers by Shoemaker (246). Microfilms were deemed more satisfactory because of greater ease in viewing pages in microfilm reading machines, better protection to the film afforded by the combination of leader, reel and carton, and the possibility of making photostats or photographic prints from microfilm.

Rider (121), arguing for the adoption of a standard size, 7-1/2 x 12-1/2 cm., for both transparent and opaque forms of microtext, discussed the principal forms then in existence and the multiplicity of sizes. He reasserted "that microfilm in reel form is an outmoded anachronism" and advocated the adoption of sheet film for purposes which could not be served by opaque forms.

In one of his summaries of the Unesco survey of microphotography (212), Bastardie (213) described the forms and dimensions of microcopies in use throughout the world. He stated:

> Each country has a preference for a different method of dealing with the same problem...microfilm in short strips is more popular in France than in England...the United States of America appears to be the land of the microcard and the microprint [!] while the Netherlands and Germany have introduced the transparent microfiche.... Microfilms are produced on transparent rolls, 8, 16, 35 or 70 mm. in width. In the United States of America, the 35 mm. reel, 30 meters (100 feet) in length, is commonly used, whereas in France [film is cut into] 23 mm. strips which take up less space and can be filled according to the decimal system.
>
> Microfiches are mainly kept in sheet form and filed... as ordinary indexcards. They are on a transparent base.... Standard sizes are: 75 x 125 mm., 90 x 120 mm., 105 x 148 mm., 105 x 150 mm., and 228 x 152 mm. Each microfiche, microcard or microprint card contains a variable number of microcopies depending upon the reduction ratio employed.

Bastardie went on to advocate the adoption of one technique and standard sizes. He recommended the opaque medium (microcards and microprint) and suggested the adoption of three sizes: 75 x 125 mm., 105 x 148 mm., 228 x 152 mm.

The various forms of microcopy are concisely described in the F.I.D. Manual (127). Microcopies as a form of document reproduction are discussed from the standpoint of their economy not only in production but also in storage and transport. The limitations of microforms also are made clear.

Formats and dimensions of microcopies are described on p. 222.3 E5-6 of the F.I.D. Manual. Here it is stated that frame sizes 9 x 12, 13 x 18, 10 x 16, 18 x 24, 24 x 24, 24 x 36, 32 x 49, 33 x 54, all in millimeters, are listed as "usual" in Europe, while frames of constant width but of variable length to suit the material being copied are the practices in the United States of America. Dimensions of sheets or cards are those used in bibliography and cataloging, 75 x 125 mm., 70 x 105 mm., 105 x 148 mm.; or in ordinary photography, 60 x 90 mm., 90 x 120 mm.; or individually chosen dimensions, 105 x 150 mm., 228 x 152 mm. In France strip films 210 mm. long of 35 mm. film covering 10 pages are usual.

Microfilm, microprint and microcards are all discussed by Fussler (131). The features of each type are described along with information on applications and relative costs. Somewhat more briefly the same author discusses sheet microfilm and composite forms, particularly those based on frames or short strips of microfilm inserted in transparent envelopes or aperture cards. Library uses of roll microfilm, sheet microfilm, microstrips, card-mounted films, microcards, microstrip, microtape, photographically produced opaque sheets and Readex microprint were indicated on a chart included in an article by Tate (132).

Ballou and Rather (247) offered the following outline of microforms: 1. Microfilm (transparent), a. Ribbon (integral), b. Sheet (integral), c. Composite forms (fragmentary); 2. Micropaper (opaque), a. Photographically printed (integral), b. Mechanically printed (integral), c. Composite forms (fragmentary). The individual types are described in regard to dimensions and other characteristics, such as the fact that sheet microfilm is often made on a heavier weight base than ribbon microfilm. Composite forms described include aperture cards and a form made by laminating short strips of ribbon film into acetate sheets.

Webb (139) enumerated such disadvantages of roll microfilm as loss of color or originals; waste of storage space; inconvenience of reeling off long lengths of film to find a desired frame; and the necessity of careful handling to avoid scratching. He stated, however, that for library use, microfilm is the standard medium and the best for "satisfying individual requests and for archival preservation." Processes of which the end product is a micro-opaque are viewed as edition processes and are discussed from this standpoint. The lack of standardization of microforms was deplored.

Microfilm and other microforms such as microcards, Minicards, and Readex microprint were described in considerable detail and discussed from the standpoint of their usefulness in government and commercial programs for the microreduction of records by Lewis and Offenhauser (143). The specific descriptions of types are contained in their third chapter (p. 29-65); however, supplementary information is to be found in other chapters. Shaw (248) in the course of discussing the problems of publication and distribution of scientific literature described Readex microprint, microcards, and sheet microfilm and discussed their potentialities in small edition publishing.

Microfilm

Reels and strips. Microfilm in the form of a ribbon rolled upon a reel or cut into short lengths after processing is the most prevalent type of microcopy, at least in the United States of America. When documentary microcopying first got under way, most of the copying was done on positive motion picture film which was sold in long lengths and stored on reels. The ribbon and the reel were taken over from the flourishing motion picture industry.

Ribbon and strip microfilm are so bound up with the development of documentary microcopying that one or the other, or both, is implied in most of the American discussions of documentary microcopying and in a considerable number of those emanating from other countries. Thus the writings on reel and strip microfilm, especially those published to about the year 1940, are approximately coincidental with the literature on documentary microcopying.

In 1938 Page and others (249) in proposing the adoption of rigid standards while library use of microforms was still young, assumed that microcopies would be made on double perforated motion picture film and they urged two forms: long lengths, say 100 feet, to be stored on reels and short strips containing up to ten pages of text. They made explicit recommendations on the length and arrangement of the strips, including multiple strips, when a document was too long to be copied on a single one.

Film strips and a system for storing them developed at the Central Medical Library Bureau of the Royal Society of Medicine were described in detail by Wilson (250) who discussed also the advantages and disadvantages of strips in comparison to rolls. He pointed out that only a little labor is required for cutting a long ribbon into strips; that strips are easily cleaned and that they facilitate the copying in color of colored illustrations (presumably because such illustrations can be photographed separately on color film).

Power (251) in a discussion of the cost of microfilm described (p. 82) strips then in use in Europe:

> At present strip film consists of strips nine inches long on single perforate film using position IIA, accommodating five frames with a half frame at each end blank. The title page and pagination of the particular strip are photographed with a supplementary lens along the top unperforated edge.

He pointed out that strip film is easy to store and use; and that readers for strip are less costly. Film strips and envelopes to contain them and carry the cataloging information developed at the Library of Congress were described in an anonymous article (252). It is stated that a maximum of 45 pages could be produced on a five-inch strip of 35 mm. film. Such advantages as the ease of reproducing strips and making enlargements from them are noted.

Seven points of superiority of microfilm over microcards and microprint were stated by Power (253) as follows: 1. lower cost, 2. more readable image, 3. reading machines more highly developed, 4. easier and more convenient to use, 5. copies may be made on demand at low cost, 6. higher reduction ratios and hence lower cost, 7. part of a microfilm cannot be misfiled or stolen. Some differences in the results which can be achieved with different widths of microfilm are indicated in a discussion by Lewis (142). He points out that the New York Times supplies 35 mm. for its published microfilm edition and uses the same width for a reference file, but uses 70 mm. film for its clipping files to get a better image.

Lewis and Offenhauser (143) described, with attention to uses and costs, filmstrips (p. 56), 16 mm. microfilm

(p. 43-47), 35 mm. microfilm (p. 47-48), 70 mm. microfilm (p. 52-55) and 105 mm. microfilm (p. 55-56). A microcopying system designed primarily for the copying of large engineering and architectural drawings, and based on the use of 105 mm. roll film which is cut after developing into 4 x 6 inch frames was briefly described (254).

Sheet microfilm (including microfiches). Microfilm in the form of sheets or cards rather than ribbons or strips is the preferred form in some European countries (120) and it has some adherents in all countries. It was probably used at least as early as ribbon film by individual scholars (175) copying books and manuscripts for their own purposes. However, the Leica camera (15) quickly became popular with scholars for copying and it used 35 mm. film strips, thus putting ribbon film and sheet film in competition practically from the beginning of the modern development of microcopying.

Van Iterson (53), inspired by the work of Bendikson in reproducing on paper from film strips side-by-side micro-images of manuscript and book pages, developed a method for producing microphotographs of nine book openings, or 18 pages, on a 13 x 18 cm. photographic plate. Presumably the plate was a glass one, but the technique foreshadowed sheet microfilm with its rows of successive images. Prints on paper were made from the glass negatives.

Hodgson (69) presented a detailed analysis of the requirements of microcopy from the point of view of librarians and research scholars and found more advantages in sheet film than in ribbon film. He pointed out the advantages of 7 x 5 inch sheets or cards, such as that they may be filed in a vertical file or bound in loose-leaf binders. They are convenient to handle and economical of space. For items only five to ten pages long, he recommended sheets the size of catalog cards. He mentioned the possibility of using metal or "some of the new cellulose products" as well as film paper for such microcopies and pointed out that both sides of opaque materials can be used for recording. Five samples showing reproductions of different types of documentary material were shown as illustrations.

In 1939, Bennett (255) summarized the findings of an investigation into "...whether the advantages of sheet microfilm for scholarly purposes are great enough to make it worthwhile to give this medium a substantial trial." The following advantages of sheet microfilm were listed:

1. A natural convenient sectionalization of the material.
2. A system of filing which mades every unit immediately accessible.
3. A means of identification which is integral with each unit and can be read without optical aid.
4. A medium more adaptable to handling and processing in small units than ribbon film.
5. A possibility of an inexpensive reading machine of limited scope and use.

A trial unit measuring 3" x 5" carrying 100 book pages at a 30:1 reduction was suggested. The author pointed out that extensive trial by commercial agencies was not to be expected because of the relatively small quantities of film used for scholarly purposes, but that a trial, fundamental research and technical developments seemed to be justified.

A camera, reader and techniques of producing microcopies on sheet film were described and illustrated by Reyniers and others (256). These experimenters used 3-1/4 x 4-1/4 inch cut film and placed the images across the film in rows with space at the top for a title visible to the naked eye. They varied the number of frames, or images, from 12 to 204, representing twice as many pages, and found that 96 were "adequate for the copying of most journal articles." They found only one film, Eastman Microfile, capable of the required resolution. However, they reported that its thin base was a disadvantage. They typed the titles on adhesive backed paper and glued them to the films. To toughen the emulsion and render the films scratch-proof, the developed films were treated by the "Vaporate process."

Mehne (93) in a comparison of roll film and sheet film for the protection of archival material in wartime, argued for sheet film, largely on the basis of greater ease in locating material. The same advantage was stressed by Redepenning (257) who said that 720 pages could be copied on ten 9 x 12 cm. cards of transparent film. He described copying techniques and portable and stationary readers.

A long two-part paper on microcopying on flat film by van der Wolk and Tonnon (119) appeared in 1950. These authors "...recount the steps by which the interest of all concerned with documentation has gradually been transferred from rollfilm via filmstrip to microcopy on the flat film."

They discuss the characteristics and the advantages and disadvantages of various types of microcopy in conjunction with their outline of historical development of the "microcard" by which term they mean a transparent piece of film in the form of a card. They describe the work and ideas of Bendikson, van Iterson, Donker Duyvis, Reyniers, Violet, Goebel, and Cordonnier in the development of this form. A short description of Rider's opaque "Microcard" is included. They describe the transparent microcard produced in The Netherlands in these terms: "...a reproduction on transparent celluloid [!] in either the format 7-1/2 x 12-1/2 cm. (international library format) or 9 x 12 cm., in Germany in the format 9 x 12 cm. only." Methods of storing and reading are briefly described.

In the second part of their paper, they defend their use of the term microcard for transparent sheet film but indicated that it may be preferable to follow the French custom of designating opaque microcopies as microcards and transparent ones as microfiches. They discuss various methods of producing transparent microcards: by placing the pages to be copied next to each other in the desired manner and photographing them at one shot; by photographing on 16 mm. ribbon film, then cutting the remaining negatives into strips and binding them; by photographing on 150 mm. film; and by photographing directly on 9 x 12 cm., or 9-1/2 x 12-1/2 cm. sheet film if the international library card format is desired. The advantages and disadvantages are discussed, in most instances, with reference to particular cameras which have been developed for producing them.

In another article in a semi-popular magazine, the same authors (258) surveyed microcopying in general and discussed ribbon film, film strips, microcards, and microfiches, but put the main emphasis on microfiches, giving special credit to Goebel and Cordonnier for their development. Pictures of Goebel's microcamera, a microfiche reader, "Microviste I," a storage cabinet, tilting camera, processing machine, and tilting machine are included. The authors conclude this article with the sentence:

> Une documentation complète, à portée de la main, facile à obtenir, facile à classer, facile à exploiter et peu couteuse enfin, c'est ce que représente la microfiche, une nouvelle ressource documentaire à qui ses avantages assureont la réussite.

Riehl (259), in an article on microfiches and microcards in documentation and the preservation of archives, described the production of microfiches with Microplex cameras, covering sizes of microfiches, techniques of photographing and developing, and costs. He concluded that the microfiche offers a more economical and more convenient solution to the problems of documentation than microfilm.

The practical realization of transparent microfiches is attributed to Goebel on p. 222.3 E 4 of the F.I.D. Manual (127). In the same place it is pointed out that although photographic film is now used for microfiche, it would be possible to use other transparent material if the number of copies wanted justified the use of a mechanical printing process. Power (260) described a sheet film system developed for the New York Times in which 70 mm. film was cut into pieces after developing. The pieces were inserted into individual transparent acetate envelopes. Identifying words and symbols were placed on the outsides of the envelopes which were then filed similarly to catalog cards. The envelopes are inserted into the reading machine and the microfilm is read without removing it.

In their description of microfiches (p. 56-57), Lewis and Offenhauser (143) mention that the Standard Register Company and the Griscombe Company, both United States of America firms, are developing sheet film equipment. Also, they state that microfiches can be read when special readers are lacking by backing the transparent film with opaque white paper and using a microcard or microprint reader. Mink (261) found many advantages to sheet film over ribbon film and other microforms. He described also and included an illustration of a special camera of microcopying on sheet film.

Shaw (248) in a discussion of various microforms from the viewpoint of their potential usefulness in the distribution of technical and scientific literature described sheet microfilm briefly and stated: "Further development of sheet microfilm as a small edition process may be anticipated...." The microform described in reference 220, produced by cutting developed 105 mm. roll film into 4 x 6 inch pieces is, of course, a method of producing a form of microfiches. Still another form, developed by the Diebold Corporation and manufactured under the name of Cumulative Microfilm is described by Stevens (151, p. 241). This form uses a transparent 8 x 5 inch sheet as a base for attaching strips cut from developed ribbon film. The strips are attached to the base sheet with cement (presumably a transparent one). The method was designed chiefly for hospital records, and its special form permits additions and withdrawals from the base sheet as desired.

Composite forms. As early as 1934, Seidell (262) proposed the mounting of film strips in apertures cut in cards. He stated:

> The cards for the master negatives on 35 mm. film, if a limit of 10 pages were to be reproduced, would require a window opening of approximately 35 cm. in length and 25 cm. wide. The cards for the 16 mm. would probably be about two-thirds this size in order to leave ample space for the individual user to write such notes and observations as he might desire. Articles of more than 10 pages would require two or more cards.

He envisioned the collection of such cards by individual scientists who would file them by subject.

Saint Rat (61) proposed cards measuring 215 x 14 mm. containing three parallel slots covered with transparent cellulose acetate. Each slot would hold a film strip 200 mm. long, and three strips would correspond to thirty pages of copied text. A reference to the original article could be written on the back of the card. Convenience in filing and storing is the object in both these arrangements; there is no suggestion of mechanical retrieval or sorting. Salchow (263) in the same year described and showed illustrations of a form of aperture, or window, card for holding pieces of microfilm.

Microcopies of documents are sometimes projected on a screen for the instruction or entertainment of audiences in which cases the microcopy is used as a lantern slide. A method of sandwiching negative or positive microfilm between two ordinary glass microscope slides to make a lantern slide, attributed to Dr. Hubert R. Alyea, was described (264). The ends of the slides are fastened together with adhesive, but the film is held only by friction, thus it is possible to salvage it for reuse if the glass becomes broken. Rider (274) described (p. 109) a do-it-yourself window card made by cutting a window 35 mm. wide in standard catalog cards. The window is transformed into a pocket by cementing cellophane back and front, the latter being cemented down after the film strip is placed in the pocket. A normal catalog entry was to be typed on the front of the card above the window. Sayce in a review of Rider's The scholar and the future of the research library (280) suggested very tentatively (p. 62) a piece of transparent film hinged to an opaque card as one form of microcard.

Williams and Rose (265) described a combination of a 3 x 5 inch plastic card and a standard 80 column punched card. The plastic card, which would bear a micro-image in most cases, covers 60 columns. The remaining twenty columns are used for a classification number and a set of randomly spaced four-digit random numbers, the two together constituting a code for retrieval. A filing system marketed by Remington Rand, Inc. under the trade name "Kard-a-Film" (266) was described in 1952. In this system, film strips are slipped into slots in the card where they are protected by transparent cellulose acetate. The strips in the card are easily changed. The system was developed for newspaper libraries and special filing operations.

Ballou and Rather (247) in a general survey of microforms described two composite forms of sheet film, Frederic Luther Unitized Acetate, which was apparently the same as the form called "Cumulative Microfilm" on p. 241 of reference 138 (see above), and Micro-Research-Card. The latter is described as a combination microfilm and punched card, measuring 5" x 8" and holding from 75 to 80 pages of text and up to 208 coding holes. They described also aperture cards and jacket cards, the first being a card with a hole in which a piece of microfilm is held, the second being a card with a "grooved opening" into which a film strip may be inserted. They stated that both types were available from the Filmsort Company, marginal punching (Keysort) and column punching (I.B.M.).

Filmsort jacket and aperture cards, manufactured by the Filmsort Division of the Dexter Folder Company, are briefly described (p. 314-316) by Lewis and Offenhauser (143) who included a picture of a Filmsort jacket. Mentioned are acetate jacket cards accommodating several frames of microfilm of one or different sizes; acetate jacket cards containing apertures for insertion of identifying notations; acetate jacket cards with paper attached to the top or bottom for notations; aperture cards of regulation card stock with acetate laminated to the paper; a transparent acetate jacket with sealed ends and slit pockets for film strips; and a self-adhesive aperture card in which the film frames or strips are mounted by pressing them to the adhesive. Punched holes for mechanical sorting are featured on some Filmsort cards.

A general survey of composite forms, including aperture cards, was written by Batchelder (267). However, he discussed them largely from the viewpoint of their applications in business and industry.

The Kodak Minicard System described by Tyler and others (268) is based on the Kodak Minicard, which is a composite form containing one or more micro-images, a slot for handling, and a code in the form of clear or opaque dots on a piece of film 16 x 32 mm. in size. Up to twelve images, each being a copy of a page as large as 8-1/2" x 14", may be accommodated on a single Minicard and still leave space for coded information to guide the sorting and selecting mechanisms. The Minicards are handled on metal "sticks", a description and picture of which are included in the paper. A stick has a capacity of 2,000 Minicards. The processes of making, duplicating, sorting, selecting and reading Minicards are described, and the capabilities of the Minicard System in documentation are summarized. Finally, units of the still incomplete System which were demonstrated in Rochester, New York, in June, 1955 are listed.

Technical details of a system used in the microcopying of geologic material, including maps, were described by Reed (269). Sheets of transparent film with a hole code on one edge and measuring 5" x 8" were used. The author also described the filing system used.

Micropaper

The idea of putting microcopies on paper rather than on film seems to have originated with Bendikson who after considerable experimental work, proposed the idea in an article in the Library journal (20) of November 15, 1933. A very short account of his work along this line is to be found also on p. 30 of the 1932/33 annual report of the Henry E. Huntington Library and Art Gallery. However, microprints on paper arranged in the form of a card were also mentioned by Björkbom (154) in an article published earlier in the same journal and in the same year. The idea was also included in a survey of photographic reproduction written by van Asperen (32) and published in 1934.

Duyvis (35) in a paper published in 1935 maintained that film in ribbon form suited the requirements of microcopying for business records and diminution of the bulk of archives but that low reduction prints on paper were better suited to copying for research. He pointed out that microcopies are inconvenient to use and that there is actually little economy in the use of film. Low-reduction copies on paper are not only inexpensive, but they can be read with the naked eye or with inexpensive loupes. Reductions of 1:3.2 or 1:4 giving reductions or surface area to one-tenth or one-sixteenth were proposed.

Bendikson began with a microfilm negative which, after development, was cut into strips. The strips were placed in rows on photographic paper and a positive was printed. This seems to be the technique Duyvis also had in mind. Bendikson advocated the use of a low-power wide field binocular microscope for reading the paper prints; Duyvis proposed reading with a loupe, such as the Bausch Lupenbrille.

In an article published in 1935, Bendikson (270) proposed a technique which would eliminate the negative microfilm. A photostat camera was to be used to make micro-images directly on paper and he described specifically a method of copying two newspaper pages on a 5 x 8 inch filing card. The disadvantages of microfilm, especially the necessity of projection, are stressed; and it is again pointed out that low reduction prints on paper can be read with a low power binocular microscope.

Van Iterson (53) made a camera which photographed nine book openings or eighteen pages on a photographic plate measuring 13 x 18 cm. Positive prints were then made on paper from the developed plate. Thus the step of cutting ribbon film into strips which were placed side by side for printing the positive was eliminated. Van Iterson's prints were read with the aid of a magnifying device. In a paper published in 1936, Bendikson (42) referred again to paper positive prints from negative microfilm and added that they were made on 5 x 8 inch pieces of glossy Azo paper. He introduced also a new idea: contact prints on paper from microfilm, the strips to be about ten frames in length and of approximately the same width as the film.

Bendikson's technique of producing paper prints from negative microfilm was described in these words on p. 118 of the Binkley Manual (45):

> Dr. Bendikson uses a Leica camera to take photographs ...on...moving picture film.... Then he lays down a few rows of these film copies side by side in a printing frame and makes from them a positive copy on paper .... It may be noted that all pages reproduced by this method are reduced to the same width, namely, one inch, the width of the available surface of the moving picture strip.

A sample page of Bendikson's microprints is included. On p. 119 of the same work there is a discussion of a recording camera, originally developed by the Folmer Graflex Corporation for meter reading which photographed directly onto a 2-1/4 inch wide strip of paper. It is stated that this camera "...will probably offer the individual scholar one of the most convenient devices for note taking."

Carruthers (43) discussed direct copies at low reductions on 70 mm. paper in comparison to microfilm. He pointed out that paper in rolls is no more convenient than film in the same form, but micropaper in the form of cards or books offers an advantage in convenience. He considered the less exacting storage requirements of paper unimportant, since large libraries would eventually be air conditioned or at least have an air conditioned storage room. He examined the factors in costs of photocopies and came to the conclusion that low reduction copies on paper would cost about the same per page copied as standard microfilm copies. His final conclusion reads: "...there would seem to be a niche in the scheme of things for 70 mm. paper without encroaching on the field of microfilm or...replacing the common photoprint."

In another presentation of contact prints on paper of microfilms, Bendikson (271) summarized their advantages, mentioning ease of making, low cost, saving of wear and tear of the negatives, only simple reading apparatus required, ease of filing. In a fuller discussion of them, the same author (73) discussed their space-saving features and relative low costs, giving somewhat more information on the latter aspect than in his earlier articles, but still not giving precise figures. He emphasized their value in libraries consulted chiefly for source materials where they could be used not only in place of the original material but of the negative copies as well.

Van Iterson (272) described again his method of making microprints by photographing eighteen octavo-size pages on an

18 x 13 cm. photographic plate, then using the developed plate to make positive prints on photographic paper. He stated that because readers had found it inconvenient to use pocket lenses, loupes, or microscopes in reading the microprints, he had modified his original scheme in favor of a maximum reduction of 6:1. These prints are read by projecting them onto an aluminum screen in such a way that the image is approximately the size of the original page. The projection apparatus is described and diagrammed.

Microcards. As shown in the preceding section, several workers were putting documentary microprints on paper in the 1930's. The term "microcard" was applied to microprints on opaque cards at least as early as 1938, for in that year a news item (273) appeared describing a system of producing miniature card catalogs, which was called "Microcard duplication." This system, reported to be under development by the Academy of Motion Picture Arts and Sciences employed cards 36 x 59 mm. in size; and it was stated that an alternative method which would print 32 cards on a 9-1/4 x 11-1/2 inch sheet, these sheets to be assembled in the form of books, was being considered. The cards were to be made by combining the techniques of microphotography and offset printing.

In the United States of America and in some other countries, the term "Microcard" now designates the type of microprint in card form advocated by Fremont Rider and defined by him as "...a standard size catalog card, having on its back a micro-text of the item catalogued on its front (274, p. 429). The primary publication on this microcard is Rider's own book, The scholar and the future of the research library. The first part of this book is devoted to a discussion of the problems presented by the geometrical growth of large research libraries and attempts made at solving these problems by "weeding."

The second and larger part of Rider's The scholar... presents microcards as a solution to the problems discussed in the first part. Microcards (the term was written "microcards" in the book) were discussed under the following subheadings: Micro-Cards: their micro-text--their catalog card format--their entry headings; Micro-cards and cataloging analysis; When the main research library consists of Micro-cards; The publication and sale of Micro-cards; Library control over Micro-card publishing; Copyright and Micro-card publication; The use of Micro-cards for certain special classes of material. Most of the discussion is concerned with administrative problems, as the chapter titles indicate; however, techniques of making microcards are described along with other matters in the chapter "Microcards--their micro-text."

Rider shows (p. 106-116) that microcards can be mechanically printed or they can be made entirely by photography. He indicated that the mechanical printing process would be the same as that used by the Readex Corporation to make Readex microprint. He describes two photographic methods, one of which requires the use of a negative made in the usual way on film, which after developing is cut into strips which are laid side by side, then printed on sensitized paper to make a positive. The other photographic method consists of photographing directly on sensitized card stock.

He goes on to point out that if the book pages to be copied can be trimmed of margins, then spread out in easy reading order and photographed at one shot, 200 to 250 "perfectly readable pages" can be put on the back of a standard catalog card at no greater reduction than the one already in use for microfilming of manuscript papers. Although he included as a frontispiece a picture of a microcard, showing a catalog entry and abstract on the front and a micro-text on the back, precise technical specifications are not given, undoubtedly because The scholar... was intended as a proposal for microcards rather than as a working manual.

Rider's book was the focal point of a symposium on the promise of microprint published in March, 1945 (275). The participants in this symposium concerned themselves largely with the administrative and research implications of microcards. However, a few technical points were covered. K. D. Metcalf discussed the technical problems of reduction and questioned whether in view of Boni's difficulties in producing Readex microprint at reductions greater than 10 or 12 diameters, the reductions indicated by Rider were possible.

Rider, in commenting (p. 180-181) on Metcalf's remarks, stated that the microcard is best suited to items not over 100 pages long and that this length is ideal for research materials because probably 95 per cent of the millions of books, articles, reports, theses, etc. are less than 100 pages long. However, he went on to say that technological experts had assured him that his book was unduly conservative in discussing the possibilities of high reduction in the future. Again, in September, 1945, Rider (276, 277) returned to this matter and reiterated that his suggestion of placing micro-images of 500 pages of an ordinary book on the back of a catalog card was intended as an indication of future possibilities.

In the September, 1945 article, Rider commented on and supplemented his previous remarks on photographic techniques. He pointed out that if two copies of a book were trimmed and spread out for photographing as described in the second paragraph above, the originals are destroyed only as bound books; in other words, they can be reassembled again as trimmed but textually intact sheets. Cementing of the pages to hold them down while being photographed would be unnecessary if a vacuum copy holder is used. He described experiments done since the writing of The scholar... and stated that by using 16 mm. film instead of 35 mm. and by measures designed to utilize all of the film area, he found it easy to put images of 50 ordinary size book pages on one card. Thus the making of the microcard is preceded by conventional microcopying. More camera time is required, but there is no need to destroy the book.

At its first meeting the Microcard Committee adopted a "proposed code for standardizing the cataloging and manufacture of Microcards." The Code (277) was published with comments. It contained 14 articles out of a projected 31 articles. Many of the articles pertain to such matters as type sizes, cataloging information, and duties of the Committee, but some describe technical specifications such as dimensions, paper stock, provision of a punched hole of stated dimensions and position. On dimensions the Code reads: "All Microcards for library use shall be of the standard international card size, 75 x 125 mm."

Besterman (278) in a review of The scholar...mentions some of the disadvantages of microcards: the physical handling of books, a pleasure, would be eliminated; browsing would be impossible, reference books and specialized periodicals would cease to be printed. To balance these he pointed out the advantages such as the saving of space and the possibility of bringing essential research materials to every scholar's desk.

Moholy (279) related Rider's microcards to suggestions made previously and mentioned the recommendations of Sayce and Donker Duyvis in particular. She stated that the advance made had been in the reduction ratio, since earlier reductions beyond 1:4 had not been encouraged. She discussed the advantages of diazo type films and papers for microcopies and stated (mistakenly): "...there is little doubt that it is a paper of the diazo family which has given microprint this new and vigorous start." She discussed also the large amount of preparatory work involved in the microcard technique and pointed out that a camera "capable of taking shot after shot, and row after row, by virtue of a mechanism within the camera itself," will eliminate the need for destroying copied books.

Sayce (280) in reviewing The scholar... referred to his own advocacy of essentially the same scheme and attributed the popularity of microfilm in rolls to the availability of such cameras as the Leica, of cinematograph film, and to the commercial success of the Recordak system. On the matter of reduction he stated that it was possible even in 1937, using "home-made" emulsions, "to reduce the text of a book to such a size that even a bulky volume of a thousand pages or more could be printed upon a card" and that since the war both Ilford and Kodak had introduced commercial "graticule" emulsions which make such reductions easier and more reliable. He pointed out the needs for a "repeating back" camera to take one thousand microphotographs on one plate, a process for printing the master negative upon the microcard ("a paper card faced with emulsion-coated metal foil or possibly even a transparent film 'hinged to the actual card'") and a simple projection microscope to serve as a reading machine.

In a letter commenting on the series of reviews just mentioned, Rider (281) discussed among other things the question of origins of the microcard and stated that the essence of the microcard is its combination of the microcard text of an item and its card catalog entry. The first issue of the Microcard bulletin (282), a periodical for dissemination of news about microcards, was published in June, 1948. The appropriate areas of application for microcards, microfilm and microprint were discussed by Price (283) who stated (p. 1): "Microcards are a new method of publication, microfilm is a method of copying."

A working party of the Scientific Information Conference of the Royal Society (244) described microcards as existing in several forms and mentioned particularly a microplaque, a transparent form used in France, and Rider's form of opaque microcards. On techniques of production they stated:

> These cards are printed from a photographically produced master, but a more flexible process would be to free microreproduction completely both from 35 mm. film and from printing and to produce opaque or transparent microcards by direct photography from the original documents.

In an article published in 1949 Parsonage (284) traced the development of the microcard from the original statement of the idea in Rider's The scholar... and surveyed its current state of development in the United States of America, showing also that up to the time this paper was written there had been no publishing of this kind of microcard in England or Europe. Keenleyside (284a) described microcards and their uses from the viewpoint of special librarians. In the same article she gave examples of publications being issued in microcard form. A short account of the origin of microcards was combined with an announcement of the beginning of production (285).

A system developed in the Color Control Department of the Eastman Kodak Company which used both microfilm and microcards in supplying research workers with literature was descibed by Kuipers (286). A master file record of 16 mm. microfilm strips is made and this is the only microrecord for material in silent demand. Actively used material and material requiring wide distribution in the organization is printed on microcards from the microstrips. The system of printing the microcards was fully described and a picture of the strip carrier for the automatic picture was included. The system includes time-saving features such as reproducible master index cards and the strip carrier mentioned, but it is at the same time flexible enough to permit making of microcard prints quickly on demand, even for the use of one researcher.

In an article addressed to chemists, Rider (287) described microcards and pointed out these features: they

> ...combine in one unit the complete text and a catalog entry, offer maximum convenience in handling, mailing and filing because they have the dimensions of standard library cards. Printed on paper stock, they are more durable and less expensive than microfilm.

He stated also that during the first year of commercial production over a million microcards had been produced. In another article (288) he discussed the use of microcards for archival materials, including office records, and described a technique for "one-copy" microcards. These were to be made by the staff of the library or archives by cutting up positive microfilm or reeled positive micropaper and pasting the strips to index cards using their card stock and non-curling mounting adhesive. This technique is described in detail. The author points out also that the method is a good one for storage and cataloging of short lengths of microfilm. In still another paper (289) he discussed the space-saving features of microcards as compared to books, with particular emphasis on administrative and economic aspects.

In a survey of the potentialities of Microcards in documentation, Kuipers (290) discussed at some length the needs for equipment that would make rapid production of microcards possible. Methods then in use appeared to him to be "largely makeshift." Specialized automatic machines were needed, but they could not be made available until sufficient demand for microcards had been built up and microcard sizes had been standardized. Original copy of standard size would also be necessary for automatic cameras and small type faces would not be needed. A comparison to the commercial production of snapshot prints was made, and it was pointed out that a photofinisher "...with continuous processing in automatic printers can make 10 snapshot prints of microcard size for the price of a single microcard."

Erickson (300), in a survey of the impact of microprint, devoted some space to microcards. He described the standard features of microcards and pointed out the new principles; "...namely, the reproduction of text at high reduction ratios, and combining of the text and catalog record on the same card." In discussing limitations of microcards, he stressed the danger of losses, the lack of a decimal arrangement of micropages on the card, the possibility that the photographic paper used meets the requirements of permanent records, the relative high cost of reproduction, and warping of the cards.

Verry (291), using information collected in a survey of microphotography in European countries advocated the adoption of microcards in Great Britain. He described in some detail potential utilization and production of microcards and other forms of microprint and gave reasons for preferring microcards.

In the F.I.D. Manual (127) it is stated (p. 222.3 E1) that the microcopies invented by Bradley Allen Fiske were the predecessors of the microcard, but on p. 221.3 E4 Rider is given credit for suggesting them in 1944 in The scholar.... On the same page the special features of microcards are described, particularly their having a catalog entry on one side and a microprint of the text of the material described in the catalog entry on the other side.

> What gives them their unique essentiality are....first, that they combine in one unit a microtext and a centralized cataloging of it, and second, that the unit employed to effect this combination is the standard size library catalog card.

Microcards are described on p. 57-59 of Lewis and Offenhauser's book (143), and are compared primarily on the basis of cost with microfilm and Readex microprint. It is stated in this article that the reduction ratio commonly used is about 1:20, thus enabling 36 to 48 pages to be copied on a standard microcard. Shaw (248) traces (p. 299) the beginning of the microcard process to Goldschmidt and Otlet's paper in volume 12 of the Bulletin of the International Institute of Bibliography (8). In the same place, the process of making microcards is concisely described: "It consists of photographing the originals in microfilm, laying up strips of microfilm, and then making contact prints on silver-halide coated cards..."

Microtape and Microstrip. Microtape, a trade name, designates positive micro-images in strip form on an adhesive backed paper. The product was described by Baptie (292) in 1947. The strips are printed from 16 mm. or 35 mm. negatives and are cut into lengths to fit standard cards. Finally, a protective layer of material is removed from the adhesive on the back and the cut lengths are pressed onto standard cards. The card built up in this way can be read in readers designed for microcards and Readex microprint. The advantage of the material is that it provides a way of putting into the form of microcard, archival and documentary material for which there is not enough general demand to justify microcard publication in the usual way.

Microstrip (293), also a trade name, designates a similar product which is used in essentially the same way. Instead of an adhesive which is made ready for use by removing a protective cover, microstrip is backed with an adhesive which requires moistening to activate it.

Readex Microprint. In 1939 Fussler (294) discussed a proposal from Albert Boni for low-cost microreproduction which had recently been put before the Executive Board of the American Library Association. This was the idea which was eventually developed under the trade name, Readex Microprint. Fussler noted that the reduction ratios would be 8 to 10 diameters, that the printing would be done by photo-offset methods, and that costs would be "extremely low." He discussed applications in rather general terms and concluded: "The technique fills a place between print, where large editions in book size are required, and microfilming, where only one or a very few copies are required."

In another early description (295) more technical details are supplied. It is stated that the first step in the process was the making of a microfilm. This was cut into 10-page strips which were assembled in 10 rows side-by-side, then a contact print was made on paper. A printing plate was made from this print. In a variation of this method, it was proposed to make the prints on diazo paper, thus eliminating the printing plate.

In an account (296) of its activities during the preceding year, the Photographic Reproduction of Library Materials Committee of the American Library Association reported that much of its attention had been given to the Boni apparatus. Describing the technique as new, the Committee indicated that both photoengraving and diazo printing were being considered, that costs would be low and that prints could be read with Readex Microprint readers. Looking ahead, the Committee reported:

> One of the most important functions of the Committee during the next few years will be to help in defining the place of this technique along with others in library service, and possibly to promote the design and manufacture of cameras that will take microcopies on bromide paper rather than on film and on rectangular pages suitable for filing rather than on film strips.

This concise description of the Readex microprint was contained (p. 69) in an article by Tennant (297) which announced the formation of the Readex Corporation: "The microprint unit for use in the Readex is a sheet of white paper, 6" x 9", containing 100 facsimile pages, each .5" x .8" in size, consecutively arranged in 10 rows of 10 pages per row, reading from left to right."

Raney (298) in a technical description of microprint as produced by the Readex Microprint Corporation described the techniques of mechanical printing and photochemical printing which have been mentioned in the preceding paragraphs and stated that the Readex Microprint Corporation was then using the diazo principle. The gist of a report by the National Bureau of Standards dated May 24, 1941, on the durability of Readex microprints is given in the same article. In his book published in 1942, Fussler (198) included a description of Readex microprint which gave about the same details on method of manufacture and characteristics of the product as in the articles already cited. He listed the claimed advantages over microfilm as: lower cost in editions of twenty-five copies or more, more convenient to use and store, and less wear in the projector.

From 1942 to 1950 there was no new promotion of Readex microprint, although it appears that the firm continued work on several major projects, particularly the microprinting of the Sabin, Church and Evans catalogs and the British Sessional Papers. Boni (299) in an article published in 1951 compared microfilm, microcards and microprint and suggested that microprint would be available only when fifty or more copies would be needed. In listing the advantages of microprint he stated among other things:

> ...consisting only of ink on paper, Microprint requires no special storage conditions other than those already provided for books and documents.... All Microprint is printed on the equivalent of 100 per cent rag paper, meeting all the specifications of the National Bureau of Standards for a minimum permanence of 300 years.

A relatively full discussion of Readex microprint was written by Erickson (300), forecasting for the process revolutionary effects in the publishing field. The author listed a number of benefits for libraries and for research in general, namely, the economies of the printing press operation; the permanence of rag paper or its equivalent; the uniform decimal arrangement of micropages on the microprint sheet; and the labeled clothbound slip cases which enable microprints to be shelved with and in the same way as books. He stressed the permanence of the paper and the color-fast printer's carbon ink used and the convenience and time-saving features of dialing a given micropage in the Readex projector. He stated that 90 per cent of the books and government documents then in print could be copied on the standard microprint sheets arranged in the decimal pattern. However, the decimal pattern would not be followed for large-size documents such as newspapers or small ones such as 3" x 5" catalog files. Readers are described and the article was concluded with mentions of several major microcopying projects being done in Readex microprint.

In their description of Readex microprint (p. 61 and 104-106), Lewis and Offenhauser (143) included this statement:

> Technical details of the process are not generally available as they relate specifically to the manner in which original microfilms are made and to the manner in which the end-use Microprint cards are produced from the microfilm. Otherwise their description of dimensions, etc. is standard.

Microlex. Microlex is similar to Readex microprint in that the micro-images are printed on both sides of a card. The Microlex card, however, is 6-1/2" x 8-1/2" in size and bears 200 micro-images on each side. The images are arranged according to a decimal scheme, but the arrangement is different from that of Readex microprint. The cards are printed photographically from a sheet film negative, Lewis and Offenhauser (130, p. 304-306) and Knight (301).

Lithoprinting in miniature. The process, or group of processes, discussed here defies an exact name and exact definition. However, the phrase is intended to designate the reproduction of documents by processes which produce some reduction in size but not an extreme reduction and of which the end product is an ink-on-paper print. The degree of reduction is less than in Readex microprint, which also produces an ink-on-paper print, and there has been no standardization of size as in Readex microprint. Photography is employed in the first steps of lithoprinting in miniature, and is the means of achieving the reduction in size, but not in the final step. The final print is made from an inked metal plate, or a substitute for the plate such as a rubber blanket.

Lithoprinting in miniature was used to produce the reading strips for the Fiskoscope, a reading device developed by Admiral Bradley A. Fiske. This device enjoyed considerable publicity in the early 1930's but most of it is outside the scope of this paper, which does not cover microcopy readers. However, the strips are described in the Binkley Manual (127) as follows:

> The frame holds a long strip of paper which can be moved up or down. The text is typewritten with short lines so that about 150 words of typescript are laid on a page doublespread. This page is then reduced seven diameters.... Each strip of paper is 2-5/8" wide and 23-1/2" long, including margins. The typescript is reduced to 1/25 of original size and is printed on both sides of the strip of paper.

A sample strip may still be found laid in some copies of the Binkley Manual.

Other schemes for reduced facsimile mentioned on p. 115-116 of Binkley's work include a plan that was proposed for publishing on rag paper by the photo-offset process a one-diameter reduction of the New York Times; an experiment by the Miller Publishing Company, which was tied in with a reading device manufactured by Bausch and Lomb, and Professor Charles G. Peters' publication of Pennsylvania State College theses in miniature typescript.

Champlin (302) described specifically the results achieved in the Pennsylvania State College program of publishing theses in reduced print:

> On the right-hand page is a thesis abstract with a linear reduction of 40 per cent and an area reduction of 64 per cent. This material may be read without the aid of a magnifying glass. On the left side is a reduction of 95 per cent in area, requiring the use of a fairly strong reading glass.

The reductions described were used in the first volume published in the series. It is noted that in the second volume the reductions in the smaller type portion were not so great. The letters were about twice as large as in the first volume. "Reading glasses are a great help in interpreting the small type, but strong eyes can read every word without help."

In an article on current and future uses of microfilm and microprint in libraries, Metcalf (98) prophesied (p. 723) that "...the greatest development in microprinting is more likely to be with photo-offset reproductions reduced by 2 to 5 diameters." In the same article he discussed briefly the Readex microprint and other reduced print schemes, including one employed for the reproduction of periodicals published in enemy countries during World War II.

Reduced print was discussed by Edwards (303) of Edwards Brothers, Inc., a leading publisher of photo-offset reproduced editions of German scientific periodicals during World War II. The advantages of photo-offset in publishing editions of 50 to 100 copies are mentioned, with emphasis on the fact that lithoprinting is closely allied to other kinds of letter-press printing insofar as the end product is concerned. Experiments then in progress in miniature offset printing are described.

> Proceeding on the principle that materials in miniature offset should be readable without the assistance of any reading device...greatest emphasis is being placed on reductions of four pages on one and nine pages on one. Depending upon generous typography and good spacing between lines, reduction of sixteen pages to one have been made and found readable by the naked eye... extreme reductions defeat the primary objective of miniature reproduction--economy and low cost for limited-demand research and reference items in a form approximating that of usual library materials. This auxiliary means of printing is designed to have greatest application in reproducing materials needed for occasional consultation and verification, not continuous reading.

Reference is made to the lithoprinted catalogs of the Library of Congress and the British Museum.

In Bastardie's (213) summary of the Unesco Survey, it is pointed out (p. E 35) that miniature facsimile is not strictly microcopy. Reduction ratios vary from 1:6 to 1:3.2, with the latter being the one advocated by the International Federation for Documentation. Facsimiles are printed and filed like index cards. They can be read without reading devices by persons with good eyesight, although some persons use a "biconvex magnifying glass." The usefulness of the method in reducing space required for documents is pointed out.

Micrometal

The durability of metal has led to several suggestions and some experimental work, but relatively little use of this class of materials as a base for microcopies. Carter (304) claimed extensive research directed toward development of metal "film" for use in record preservation. He stated (p. 358) that any document could be reproduced by his process "...with minute faithfulness..." He claimed development of a 35 mm. projector for projecting from the metal film. Among the advantages of metal film as seen by Carter (p. 361):

> Metal film is permanent, fadeless, and practically indestructible. Metal film does not weigh any heavier than cellulose acetate film. Metal film is positively incombustible, will not cost any more than cellulose acetate film, and will give pictures or sound equal to cellulose film. Metal film will outwear and outlast cellulose film 100-1.

Peters (305) described in considerable detail his experimental developmental work with metal film for record preservation. He conceived the idea of a thin metal film about 1912 and made several small reels. Later, stimulated by Dr. Jacobs, President of Oglethorpe University, he returned to metal film as a medium for preserving documentary records for the Crypt of Civilization at Oglethorpe University. In the process used for this purpose, the document was first photographed on 35 mm. cellulose acetate film. A print of this film was made on the metal film; and in a series of ingenious steps which included the deposit of new metal in an intaglio surface produced by etching, a black image on a white background, both the image and the background being metal, was produced. Methods of further preparing both the acetate film and the metal film for storage in the Crypt are described. No information is given on the cost of the process.

Quality Factors

General. The quality of micro-images of documents would naturally be of concern from the very beginning of the use of microcopying for record preservation and documentation, since a micro-image of written matter is of little value if it cannot be read. Nevertheless, published writings on the subject do not begin to appear for several years after the beginning of the modern development of microcopying. A paper by Gillot (36) which discussed in a semi-technical style problems of reduction, enlargement and readability of micro-images on 35 mm. film appeared in 1935.

The quality of images was one of the principal points covered in a symposium by Kuhlman (38) on the preservation of newspapers on film. Participants in this symposium stressed needs for information on the durability of film records; the chemical and physical properties of cellulose acetate film and of photographic emulsions; specifications for photographing and processing which would serve as guides to obtaining the most usable and durable product; and the need for fine grained films and methods of processing them so as to secure sharp reproductions. Needs only were pointed out; there was no attempt at setting up tests or standards, although it was implied that the National Bureau of Standards would make the necessary studies.

Tate (65) discussed (p. 20) the influence of the film, or more precisely the color response of the emulsion, on the quality of microcopies. He pointed out that copying could be done on color film, or on monochrome film responsive to color. Also, by choosing film with suitable color response and using suitable filters and lighting a copy could be produced more legible than a faded and stained original. Much the same information is included in another paper by Tate (72). However, in this second paper he lists four kinds of microphotographs: 1. full color, 2. full tone, 3. contrast, and 4. corrected.

> The full color microphotograph is used to reproduce an original..as it appears to the human eye. A full tone microphotograph preserves in monochrome the relationship of the tones of an original as viewed by the human eye. A contrast copy attempts to obtain the maximum degree of separation between the background and the... textual matter. In some cases this may overlap into the fourth classification, that of a corrected copy which is employed to reproduce or eliminate desirable or undesirable portions of an original.

Bendikson (73) carried out an experiment designed as a test of the quality of reproduction obtainable with two kinds of film, ordinary positive motion picture film and Eastman Microfile, at reduction ratios of 10:1, 20:1, 30:1, 40:1, and 50:1.

Quality of the developed images was tested by making enlargements on paper, by examining photomicrographs of sections of film negatives and by microscopically examing contact prints. The limit of reduction of both kinds of film appeared to have been reached at the 50:1 ratio. The images in the positive motion picture film were less legible at the 50:1 ratio than those on the microfilm film, but all prints "retained a certain degree of legibility." As a result of the experiment, the author recommended that Microfile film rather than positive motion picture film be used when it is intended to make contact prints on paper of films produced at ratios of reduction as high as 40:1 or 50:1.

In a survey (182) of the status of microphotography in 1938, it was stated (p. 155):

> There is as yet no concrete definition of quality in microfilming.... A crude working definition of an 'ideal' microfilm is, namely, one which can be enlarged back to original size on paper without noticeable loss in sharpness at normal reading distances. In determining the ratio of reduction, therefore, it is imperative that this definition be considered. It is not always necessary to achieve an 'ideal' result, for copies of originals may serve quite well for some purposes in a less perfect form.

Quality and costs were discussed by Case (306) who pointed out that quality is not important in microcopies made in lieu of interlibrary loan but is of primary importance in archival films. He outlined five factors in achieving quality and low cost: equipment, film operator's skill, expert processing and good projection apparatus, then discussed each factor in detail. Requirements in the camera for producing high quality microfilms are: absolute rigidity; a high quality long-focus; anastigmat achromatic lens with resolving power at least equal to that of the finest grain film; means for sharp focusing at all degrees of reductions; means to hold the film absolutely flat in the focal plane. Film requirements are stated as: safety, contrast, latitude, uniformity, fine grain, and panchromatism. It is pointed out that ordinary safety positive film meets all but the last two requirements and that such a film as Eastman Microfile meets all six.

In the same article processing for films of good quality is outlined as follows:

> After selecting the proper formulae required by the film used, and acquiring pure tested chemicals, the steps in processing consist of the following: 1. Mixing chemicals (accurately). 2. Temper the solution. 3. Develop test strip to determine developing time. 4. Develop (agitate film throughout). 5. Rinse or stop bath. 6. Fix (2 fixing baths are advisable for archival films). 8. Dry. 9. Inspect thoroughly. 10. Test for residual hypo content.

It is stated that processing should be carried on in an air-conditioned room supplied with filtered air to avoid dust on the film.

The steps in making positive prints are described as:

> Take density readings throughout negative to determine best printing time. 2. Mark points at which light changes should be made to correct variations in density. 3. Clean negative thoroughly. 4. Print. 5. Process positive as above for negative, except, of course, with positive developer. 6. Inspect positive. 7. Test for residual hypo content.

Holmes (307) in a paper on quality dealt principally with photographic equipment and technique. He covered in some detail such requirements as a rigid camera and camera mounting, a precision lens with a resolving power of at least 125 lines per millimeter at 20 diameters minification and a variable light source free from hot spots. Pointing out the importance of the sensitive material used, he stated that several film emulsions had been developed for documentary reproduction and that the characteristics of these included speed, contrast, fine grain, color sensitivity, halation protection and resolving power up to 135 lines per millimeter. Discussing the influence of techniques, he stressed the importance of frequent use of an exposure meter; use of contrast filters when copying documents on colored paper or written in ink; and care in processing particularly in regard to control of the temperature of solutions, accurate timing, sufficient washing and cleanliness.

In a paper addressed to scientists interested in making microcopies for their own purposes, Reid (197) included the information that a soft gray background in microfilm negatives is easier on the eyes than a dense black, therefore films should not be developed to a high density and contrast.

Minimum standards of quality enunciated by the National Bureau of Standards for permanent record microfilms were stated in full (308). These standards provided that such film should be of the cellulose acetate type sensitized with a gelatin halide emulsion and that after processing it should be thoroughly washed. Tests and standards for flexibility, acidity, relative viscosity and nitrogen content were specifically described. The maximum permissible hypo content was stated as .005 milligrams per square inch of film, determined by the Ross-Crabtree or the Crabtree silver nitrate test.

Writing as a bibliographer, Jackson (87) named many limitations of microfilm as a substitute for actual books. Noting that "exact verisimilitude is of utmost importance" in bibliographical study, he noted such faults in film reproductions as coarsening of lines, exaggerated contrast, lack of color differentiation, and the occasional introduction of marks or changes of tone not in the original. He deplored also the failure of films to give the "feel" of the original and to give information on stitching, age of leather bindings, changes of paper, facsimile leaves, etc.

Flemer (309) described a method for testing the strength of used developer solution which would contribute to the production of microfilms of uniform density. The method was based on the use of three samples of developer, one freshly prepared, one known to be almost exhausted, and one of an age between these extremes. Three negatives, exposed alike, are developed in the three solutions at uniform time and temperature. A second set of three negatives is then developed to the density of the darkest negative of the first set and times required are noted on the first samples. By comparing a negative developed under standard conditions in a developer of unknown strength with the three samples, the time necessary for full development can be estimated. A device for producing a standard test negative is described and illustrated.

In the ninth chapter of his book, Fussler (198) briefly discussed standards of quality and stated that there is often justification for two standards of work but there should be no compromise with quality in making microfilm for permanent use. He mentioned as quality points: quality of the film base, resolution, lighting of the original document, film density, grain, residual hypo, spacing of images, length of leaders and trailers, spooling, packaging, and identification. Techniques for checking resolution, density, and laboratory conditions in the production of microfilms of good quality were described by Garver (235). Four grades of inspection of microfilms and the procedures for each are fully described in a War Department Technical manual (105). The need of inspection is discussed and the tendency for defects to be concentrated due to faulty equipment or inexperienced operators is pointed out.

Higgins and Jones (310) in a technical article on sharpness in photographic images showed that resolving power does not correlate well with sharpness judgments. They stated (p. 290):

> ...from the standpoint of sharpness, the important property of the image is the acutance of the edges of the lines which are just resolved by the eye.... Resolving power is therefore a limiting condition which does not furnish information as to the sharpness of detail which is well resolved by the eye.

They did not relate their findings particularly to microfilm images but discussed photographic images in general.

Verry (311) studied the problems of response to color in document copying. He showed that the sensitivity of modern photographic emulsions varies with the type of light used and that certain colors do not reproduce as expected. He summarized in a chart facts about these colors and their reproduction responses.

Factors influencing the quality of microfilm images were discussed in a long, detailed paper by Rudd (312). He listed the requirements of lenses for microfilm cameras and enlargers as freedom from aberrations, coated surfaces, resolving power of at least 100 lines per millimeter, a flat field and good definition over the entire field. He pointed out the sharpness of fine detail recorded or the legibility of an enlarged reproduction is a better criterion of lens quality than resolving power. Possible causes of loss of legibility in micro-images and in reproductions made from them include dirt on the lens, poor focusing or vibration during exposure. The bad effects of smoky or opalescent coatings on the lens and the speed with which such coatings form under certain common conditions are discussed. A method of inspecting and cleaning a lens is described.

Essential characteristics of film for negative microcopying

are given as high resolving power, good image sharpness, extremely fine grain, moderate emulsion speed and high contrast, or gamma. Because microfilm is a high-contrast material, exposure must be carefully controlled. The author recommended changing camera exposure to adjust to varying photographic quality of the document so as to produce a roll which can be printed off at a constant printing exposure.

The two basic problems of exposure: the copying of documents of varying contrast or brightness range, and the copying of lines of varying widths, are discussed and related to practical microcopying of documentary material. It was stated that small changes in exposure produce disproportionately greater changes in the density of the negative due to the high contrast characteristics of the emulsion. Underexposure affects legibility because both the text and the background are reproduced as shades of gray while overexposure fills in the narrow parts of letters and, furthermore, necessitates an above-normal exposure in enlarging which, in turn, produces a spreading of the broad lines of letters. Excess exposure also reduces line width while underexposure gives a wider line. The optimum exposure for a document containing both fine and broad lines is a compromise.

The author suggested the classifying of documents to be copied into five categories on the basis of contrast and line width. The first category--for which a relative exposure of 100 per cent was recommended--is comprised of printed books, periodicals, typewritten matter and "any dense black moderate-sized printing or writing," and thus included the majority of material types copied in libraries or for library purposes; the second category contained fine or small printing, lightly typed letters and writing done with a soft pencil; the third, pencilled engineering drawings, somewhat faded printing, graphs with thin colored lines, and very fine printing; the fourth, lightly handwritten manuscripts and drawings and poorly printed, faint documents; the fifth, paper-negative type copies, such as photostats. Relative exposure factors and negative density values are given for each group. Explicit directions are given for finding optimum negative exposures for materials in the five group classifications.

In summing up, the author mentioned also the importance of periodically measuring light intensity, inspecting and maintaining equipment, cleanliness, and focusing of camera and enlarger lenses.

Two examples of deteriorated record microfilms, one case of deterioration having been due to the unintentional use of nitrate film, the other to poor processing, led to the initiation by the Library of Congress in April, 1954 of a regular program of testing samples of microfilm acquired from outside sources. The program was described concisely by Holmes (133) and more fully by Clapp and others (313). It was designed to determine whether the film was of safety or flammable base; whether it contained enough residual hypo to affect its life; and whether the image definition was satisfactory. Sampling and testing procedures are described and the results of the program during the first six months are summarized. Although the percentage of reels rejected was small--0.2 per cent for inadequate definition and 2.5 per cent for excess residual hypo--relatively high percentages of the films supplied by some processors were rejected for excess residual hypo, and a single source accounted for more than half of these rejects.

On the basis of this testing experience, the authors drew the general conclusions that a majority of processors were supplying adequate film, but that film from unknown or sporadic suppliers must be tested. They state that the question of spending money on film testing is one for administrative decision and suggest that the nature of the material filmed should be one factor in the decision. From this viewpoint four categories of microfilm acquisitions are outlined (p. 591):

> 1. Unique copies: no other negatives or positives and the original material destroyed; 2. positives backed up by negatives maintained under controlled conditions, e.g., most commercially filmed newspapers; 3. negatives or positives of which multiple copies of positives exist; and 4. negatives or positives supported by adequately protected and reasonably accessible original material.

The authors urge that libraries insist upon a warranty from purveyors and suggest that a national testing laboratory be set up for making appropriate tests on a cost basis for microfilm and other photographic materials. Finally, they describe technical procedures of tests for distinguishing nitrate from safety film; image definition; and residual hypo. The Library of Congress test program was mentioned in the Report of the librarian for 1955, where it is stated (p. 12) that of 2,653 reels tested during the year, 408 were returned to suppliers, in most instances because of residual hypo.

Ballou and Rather (247) pointed out that the same standards are not required in microcopies designed for everyday use as in archival microcopy. They suggested three terms of durability: 10 to 25 years, 10 to 50 years, and over 50 years, and suggested that the producer of the microfilm (that is, the photographer-processor) should be informed about the term of durability required. Extending the same idea, the librarian should be aware of the effects of careless processing.

Van Gieson (315) discussed microfilm quality primarily from the viewpoint of the processor. He listed as quality factors: subject matter, exposure, camera optics, degree of reduction, characteristics of film used for the negative, printer or reader optics, characteristics of the film or paper used for reproduction, "plus the man on the job." Pointing out that a film's ability to render detail must sometimes be sacrificed to get a clean-up reproduction of a soiled original, he indicated that both types of reproduction, that which reproduces all detail and that which minimizes detail to suppress the blemishes of the original, can be microfilms of quality. The film characteristics necessary to achieve these extremes are discussed and represented graphically. He showed also that they can be achieved with the same film by using a low activity developer for one result, a high activity developer for the other, or by varying the developing time. An alternative method is to select film with characteristics that will lead to the desired rendition of detail.

In discussing the effects of grain, Van Gieson pointed out that grain size is a factor of lesser importance in the quality of 35 mm. and 70 mm. micro-images, but at the high reductions usually employed on 16 mm. film, grain size affects image quality. Scattering of light within the emulsion, more of a problem in coarse grained films than in fine grained ones, also reduces image sharpness. Fine lines register at a higher density than broad lines of the same original blackness, because of light scattering in the emulsion. Overexposure reduces line widths and increases density, while underexposure has opposite effects on line width and density.

Lewis and Offenhauser (143) treat various aspects of microfilm quality. On p. 40-41 of their book they describe testing procedures and the application of statistical quality control to microfilm testing, without, however, going into the mathematical aspects of the latter. They recommend constant, systematic testing:

> ... the user should take from the original, after it is developed, short samples in the form of test clippings from the ends of finished films; such clippings should provide special exposures for process check by means of such tests. The clippings should be tested for all required attributes by a competent testing organization....
>
> ... the commercial testing laboratory will apply the principles of statistical quality control... In the beginning it will be necessary to do considerable testing.... A clipping sample should be taken from every roll, or at least for every day's output. A clipping sample should also be taken from all copies made, or all intermediate copies required to produce the desired end-use copies. If a sample from each stage in the process is available for each day, it becomes possible to locate the source of the trouble and to specify how to correct it should an unsatisfactory product be produced .... The percentage of product to be tested depends upon the quality level of the product; when the quality level is consistent and high, the amount of testing required becomes small. The collection of test data is necessary to determine just what the quality level is; if the quality level proves to be high, the amount of testing required can be reduced as dictated by the mathematical criteria...

The quality of sharpness (to be distinguished from resolving power) in micro-images is discussed on p. 96-98 of Lewis and Offenhauser's book. They state that no standard method for numerically evaluating this quality has been adopted, but they do describe a technique used to evaluate it in photographic research laboratories. The technique is based on the use of a microdensitometer and a checkboard pattern of black and white squares. The microdensitometer is made to traverse the boundary between a black square and a white square while measuring the density of microscopically small areas. A curve is traced, the shape of which is an indication of the quality of sharpness of the micro-image. For users of microfilm, the authors recommend evaluation of sharpness by visual tests of developed microfilms at three times the magnification used in the microfilm readers and comparison with a checkerboard test pattern at the same degree of magnification.

The same authors discuss (p. 98-99) the loss of detail in successive generations of copy as when a negative film is used to print a positive, another copy is made from the positive, etc. They indicate that a loss of detail of approximately 30 per cent can be expected in each generation. On p. 130-136, they present a concise discussion of the factors affecting image quality in practice. This discussion was based in part on a paper by Rudd (312), but includes additional information on the effects of vibration of the camera, on atmospheric dust as a limiting factor in large reduction ratios, on the importance of specifying the number of copy generations anticipated when discussing reduction ratios. They point out also the need for a statistical study of degradation of microfilm image quality. Reference is made to an elaborate statistical study of the quality of television pictures made by the Bell Telephone Laboratories and it is suggested that the same levels of degradation might be found in reproductions of micro-images.

In their descriptions of processing of microfilm, Lewis and Offenhauser devote two paragraphs (p. 185) to "green film" a quality characterized by soft, even sticky emulsion. They state that it is caused by too rapid drying in processing, and argue against "film-preservative processes" as a way of correcting green film.

That any photographic-copying process causes some degradation of image sharpness was pointed out (p. 249) by Stevens (151) who suggested the following subject standards:

Standard	Description of copy
Perfect	Degradation only just detectable. Copy suitable for students of printing.
Excellent	Degradation in no way affecting legibility. Copies suitable for prolonged study by scholars or research workers.
Commercial' quality	Degradation obvious but copies still easily legible without eye-strain.
Decipherable	Degradation pronounced. Identity of individual letters doubtful. Words can be mostly read but some have to be guessed from the context.

The same author discussed (p. 250) the problem of contrast, pointing out that moderate contrast gives latitude in exposure and easier working tolerances than a high process, and that the greatest tolerance is obtained when the black of the document being copied is recorded as not quite black and the white as light gray. In a discussion of the necessary compromise between a heavy exposure giving high contrast and a lighter one that will keep the lines of letters open, he included a graph in which exposure is related to film density and a curve is marked to indicate the low-contrast region most suitable for documentary copying at high ratios of reduction. Other points related to exposure which affect image quality discussed by this author include control of the brightness of illumination and prevention of creeping of pages during the period of exposure.

Reduction ratios. Ratios of reduction in microcopying are of interest to photographic technicians and to librarians, though from different viewpoints. Metcalf (46) in discussing the problem from the librarian's point of view related ratio of reduction and ratio of enlargement in projectors or readers. He mentioned as factors in the problem, the film emulsion, quality of the photography, the size of the letters being copied, the width of the film and the position of the image on the film.

The Binkley Manual (45) contains a variety of information pertinent to reduction ratios. A table entitled "Thresholds of legibility in reductions of typescript and newsprint" on p. 116 shows whether newsprint and pica typescript at various selected reductions can be read with the unaided eye, a reading glass, or projector. This table indicates that newsprint reduced twenty diameters is difficult to read and that reduced more than twenty diameters is impossible to read even with a projector or reading machine! A scale of legibility appearing on p. 123 describes five qualities of legibility:

> A...all letters distinct; B...edges of letters begin to blur; C...tops of the 'o's,' 'd's,' 'p's,' and 'b's,'; D...almost illegible. The openings of 's's,' 'o's,' 'd's,' etc. are blotted solid. Separate words can be deciphered but not read; E...absolute illegibility.

Results of photographing 7-point newsprint at various reduction ratios with various cameras are summarized in terms of this scale. Various experiments with reduction and enlarging back to the original or different size are described and the results are printed in facsimile.

Binkley went on to discuss (p. 121) reduction ratios in relation to the grain of film emulsion and states that although letters begin "to blur over" below twenty diameters of reduction, fairly legible enlargements can be made of 36:1 negatives if the photography has been done carefully. He proposed a measure of reduction based on 7-point newsprint, pointing out that type of this size can be satisfactorily reduced 16 diameters, the same material and process should make reductions of 25 to 32 diamteters feasible for 14-point type.

He listed as factors limiting the reduction ratio the body of the type (whether heavy or light), the spacing of letters, the whiteness of the paper, the blackness of the ink and the sharpness of the edges of the letters. Despite such qualities, however, every page can be equated with newsprint so that "newsprint reduced by x diameters is the microphotographic equivalent of the other page reduced y diameters." He stated (p. 122) his conclusion that a reduction ratio of 18 diameters of 7-point newsprint, equivalent to 36 diameters of 14-point type, was well within the capacity of most film, apparatus and workmanship.

Sayce (316) discussed reduction ratios in a paper on standardization. According to him (p. 141), there was no apparent loss of detail when ordinary letterpress was reduced 12 diameters, but at 18 diameters the loops of "a's" and "e's" became filled in, and at 25 to 40 diameters, letterpress became more or less illegible according to the size of the original type. He described a reduction of 12 diameters as ideal and stated that it was not desirable to exceed 18 diameters. Townsend (317) stressed the importance of obtaining an adequately high resolving power at each step in the microcopying processing, especially in the copying of materials which may not be available for recopying. She pointed out that poor contrast or density can usually be corrected, but that a poor resolution of the image cannot be made better in later steps; rather there is a degradation of sharpness with each step. Bendikson (73) stated a preference for low reduction ratios on two counts: convenience and better results in the hands of photographers with little experience. However, he described the method and results of an experiment designed to test the quality of images at ratios of reduction from 10:1 down to 50:1. This experiment--summarized more fully on p. 78 of this report--indicated that legible enlargements could be made from micro-images produced at a 50:1 reduction.

In a review of the state of microcopying in 1939, Sayce (85) mentioned (p. 77) that his own experiments with high-resolution emulsions (apparently emulsions of his own formulation) indicated that it was technically possible "...to photograph as many as 2,000 pages upon the area of a postcard..." Rahts (193) stated that there is no generally known method of measurement for the resolving power of film, then went on to describe film qualities that contribute to good resolving power such as a clear emulsion, a steep contrast curve, freedom from inner and outer halation, and uniformity.

Reductions possible in microcards were the subject of some controversy because some readers misunderstood Rider's remarks on this point as published in his The scholar and the future of the research library (274). He forecast reduction ratios which would make it possible to copy 500 pages of a book of ordinary size onto a microcard the size of a standard catalog card, but included as a frontispiece a picture of a microcard with only 100 pages copied on it. Metcalf (p. 171 of ref. 275) questioned whether the technical problems of reproducing even 100 pages in such a small space had been solved and cited the experience of Readex microprint which had found it impractical to use reduction ratios greater than 10 or 12 diameters in its offset printing process. However, Metcalf did indicate that higher reductions were possible by photographic reproduction on smooth sensitized paper.

Rider, in a reply (p. 180 of ref. 241) to the comments on his proposed reduction ratios, reiterated that the card shown as a frontispiece to his book was made by photographic methods and that he did not know whether such a high reduction was feasible by the Readex microprint method. In the same discussion, he pointed out that high reduction ratios would be unnecessary in copying most research materials on microcards because research documents are usually less than 100 pages long.

In a review of Rider's The scholar and the future of the research library, Sayce (280) referred to his own experiments in microcopying at high reductions. He stated that with "home-made" emulsions it was just possible in 1937 to copy a book of one thousand or more pages upon a card, but that "graticule" emulsions introduced by the Kodak and Ilford firms since World War II enabled reliable and easy achievement of such reductions. He included in his paper an illustration of a standard catalog card 7.5 x 12.5 cm. ruled for one thousand page spaces, a 2 x 3 mm. micropage, an enlargement of this page to readable size, and a portion of an enlargement of the 2 x 3 mm. micropage to the size of the original. He went on to say that the fundamental and optical problems of such reductions had been solved but that suitable cameras, printing processes and reading instruments remained to be developed.

The introduction of Philips M. D. (metal-diazonium) film with a resolving power of one thousand lines per millimeter prompted a paper by van Alphen and Dippel (202). These authors discussed the factors in recording a micro-picture, then making it legible by projection or enlargement. They compared the resolving power of Philips M. D. film with Kodak Verichrome, 35 mm. positive safety film, 35 mm. Panatomic X, high contrast positive safety; 35 mm. Microfile; and with miniature printing and offset techniques. They showed that the resolving power of the new material far exceeded the optical limitations of camera lenses, microscope objectives and projection apparatus. They stated that if the microcopies were to be projected by the light of tungsten lamps the micro-picture could not be smaller than 4 x 6 mm., making it possible to place about 400 such pictures on a 9 x 12 cm. sheet; but if they were to be read with a reading microscope, 7,000 such pictures could be put on a 9 x 12 cm. sheet, equivalent to copying the Encyclopedia Britannica on three such sheets.

Siedentopf (108) in a general survey of microcopy in documentation stated that the best microcopies for purposes of reproducing additional copies are those reduced 1:20 or 1:30. He pointed out that documentary material can be copied at reductions as high as 1:300, but the microcopies are delicate, and easily damaged by scratches. Oosterloo (205), also inspired by a demonstration of Philips M. D. film, discussed reduction ratios, resolving powers of commercially available films, and the spheres of application of 1:26 reduction ratios and higher ratios such as 1:45. What can be accomplished at these ratios in the way of copying large numbers of pages of specified size on 6 x 9 cm. and 9 x 12 cm. sheet film is thoroughly discussed. An extended technical discussion of photographic reproduction and reduction was rendered in a paper by Lubeck (318). In the light of the basic considerations, this author recommended reduction ratios of 1:16 and 1:20 and a format of 9 x 12 cm. for microcopies.

Power (117) described tests of microfilms made at a 20:1 reduction ratio of journal pages set in 8-point type, the image positioned so that a double spread of pages ran across the width of 35 mm. film.

> This film when carefully prepared, projects an image on the screen that is clear, sharp and readable with either an Eastman Kodagraph reader at 22 x (times) enlargement, an Eastman MPE reader at 19 x, or a Griscombe reader at 25 x. Subscript figures in 4-point type are legible and illustrations are satisfactory.

Shaw (319), in an analysis from the management viewpoint of potentialities in the mechanization of bibliography, included data showing the effects of various reduction ratios on space required for the copy; for example, (p. 205)

> If 300 power reduction ratios reported experimentally were developed for routine use, then microcards would store...250 octavo pages in 0.0017 cubic inches; and at 300 diameters 16 mm. microfilm in one-hundred foot rolls and the Rapid Selector would require considerably less space for storage of 100,000 words than would microcards.

A table on p. 208 summarizes comparative data from the standpoint of storage efficiency for 35 mm. microfilm, microcards, 16 mm. microfilm and 300-diameter reduction microfilm. Quality factors pertaining to legibility are not discussed in this paper.

The Committee on Duplication of the American Library Association published a warning to libraries about poor quality in microfilm copies of newspapers. It pointed out that reduction ratios greater than 16.5:1 do not result in low quality if the work is carefully done on fine grain film. However, film copies examined of newspapers at reductions of 19 or 20 diameters showed varying density within frames, especially on corners, and the centers of small type filled in. It was recommended that librarians test newspaper microfilm by enlarging some frames to full size and that good quality be demanded, particularly when the microfilm will be used to make copies for research, etc.

Resolving power of photographic lenses and films is discussed on p. 91-96 in Lewis and Offenhauser (143). They describe standard tests and test charts and point out the effects of conditions under which a test is made on the results. Among the factors mentioned are the line-to-space ratio of the test object, the contrast of the test object, the level of illumination under which the test images are examined, the chromatic characteristics of the light used to make the test exposure, conditions of development, and the grain characteristics of the film. The effects of each of these factors are concisely described. This discussion is concluded with these sentences (p. 96):

> Usually the conditions of tests by suppliers of equipment, materials and services and the actual conditions of use is quite poor. For this reason, manufacturers' ratings of resolving power are frequently little more than a qualitative guide....

In a discussion (p. 133-136) of certain practical aspects of reduction ratios, these authors state that a limit of 5 lines per millimeter may be taken as the limit of resolving power for the unaided eye when viewing print of high quality under advantageous viewing conditions and suggest a resolution of 5 lines per millimeter multiplied by the reduction ratio as a rule-of-thumb in assessing microrecording materials. A microcopy with such a resolution would be suitable for making further copies, while one with half of it might be readable though not sharp enough for making copies. In the light of this rule, the authors examine the reduction ratios suggested in the section on microcopying in the F.I.D. Manual (127) and point out the necessity for specifying the number of copy generations anticipated when specific reduction ratios are given.

The Kodak Minicard system (267) is an interesting example of the use of a high reduction ratio. The reduction ratio employed is 1:60 and legible prints can be made from sixth generation copies (Lewis and Offenhauser (143), p. 60). Presumably the processing is carefully controlled to achieve these extraordinary results.

Disadvantages of high reduction ratios from the photographer's viewpoint were discussed by Stevens (151), who pointed out (p. 247) that the higher the reduction, the higher the required resolving power of the emulsion, and the lower its speed. A slow emulsion requires longer exposure times and does not have the tolerance of a faster emulsion. A lower tolerance leads to more flaws, and since more images are recorded on a given unit at high reductions, spoiling of only one image wastes more work than would be wasted at a lower reduction ratio. The author concluded both on these grounds and in consideration of the user's viewpoint that micro-images should be as large as is consistent with the aims of the process; in other words, high reduction ratios are justified only when there is a genuine need to reduce the bulk or weight of the microcopy. In discussing very high reduction, Stevens stated (p. 255-257) that they cannot be made by present-day commercial methods and that it has never been demonstrated that they can be made economically in large quantities. He goes on to say that when the advantages of microscopic documents are sufficient, the work should be organized so that every image is inspected to prevent a high proportion of rejected images in order to cause a minimum of inconvenience.

Residual "hypo." The deleterious effects upon photographic images of sodium thiosulfate ("hypo") had attracted attention before the problem became important in documentary microphotography. The Crabtree-Ross test (321), which is still the standard test for residual hypo in developed film and is widely used in the testing of permanent record films, was published in a professional journal of the moving picture industry before there was much, if any, use of microfilm for preservation of documents. In fact, in a National Bureau of Standards report by Kimberley and Scribner (29), film was viewed as an unstable medium on several counts, among which was the residual effects of the reagents [not specifically named in the report] used in developing (p. 25):

> After exposure the film is chemically treated to render the emulsion insensitive to further exposure to light. As a result of this chemical treatment, small quantities of reagents are left upon the surface and in time cause deterioration of the emulsion, and this results in a gradual diminishing and eventual total extinction of the image. This occurs even though the most careful treatment is accorded the negative.

Hill and Weber (330) described test methods for determining folding endurance, pH, copper number, relative viscosity and residual hypo of motion-picture film used at the National Bureau of Standards, then described the properties (as determined by these tests) of film suitable for the recording of records of permanent value. On residual hypo, they stated: "Developed film shall be free from sodium thiosulphate (hypo) as indicated by the mercuric chloride test..."

Test methods developed by the National Archives and the National Bureau of Standards for determining the quality and condition of finished films offered to archivists and librarians for custody were described by Gibson and Weber (322) and published in 1938. In contrast to established methods which required fairly large samples of the film being tested, these were semi-micro methods adaptable to test specimens as small as 7 mg. in weight which could be removed from the film with a hand punch. The tests provided for determination of acidity, viscosity and residual hypo.

In an important contribution to the subject of hypo elimination, Crabtree and others (234) discussed the various factors which affect the rate of fading of photographic images and the washing out of hypo from films and papers. Their paper was concerned principally with the elimination of hypo from prints on paper, but they included some useful information on its elimination from film negatives. In passing, they pointed out that fine grained emulsions tend to fade more rapidly than coarser grained emulsions and that fine grained positive transparencies are more susceptible to fading than images in fast negative emulsions. A chronological, annotated list of hypo eliminators is appended to their paper.

The technical literature of photography abounds in papers on hypo elimination and tests for residual hypo. No attempt will be made to cover this photographic literature in this report; however, mentions will be made of several papers on these topics which have appeared in the professional journals of librarianship, even though most of them were derived from technical papers published in the photographic literature. Fussler (323) in his Library journal column gave explicit procedures for the Crabtree-Ross test for residual hypo in finished films and the potassium permanganate test for photographic prints, which is made while the prints are being washed. In the following issue of his column (324), he described procedures of the Clark and Jelley tests for hypo in films and papers while being washed, and the sodium sulphide test for completeness of fixation of photographic images. He referred briefly to the use of conductivity meters in testing wash water for hypo. In two later issues (325) he summarized Crabtree, Eaton and Muehler's paper (234) on hypo elimination, giving special emphasis to their test procedures.

Residual hypo determination was a principal factor in a method for predicting permanence of photographic images issued as an American Standard (326) in 1948, and a later publication (327) described an approved method of determining it in processed photographic papers. The Library of Congress testing program for films from outside suppliers described by Clapp and others (313) included testing for residual hypo. Excess hypo was the leading cause for rejection of films in the first year of operation of this program. The Kodak Hypo Estimator is described (p. 186) by Lewis and Offenhauser (143) who pointed out that it is an easy method to use but that the Crabtree-Ross test is more suitable for precise determinations.

Durability and stability. Even as late as 1934 film was not considered a suitable medium for the preservation of records. In a report issued in that year by the National Bureau of Standards (29) the many characteristics of film that seem to indicate a lack of permanence were discussed and it was stated (p. 25): "... it is doubtful if any great increase in permanence of the records would result from the copying of manuscripts or similar material from impermanent paper upon photographic film." The need for tests by the Bureau of Standards that would throw light on the durability of film was one of the points made in a symposium on the preservation of newspapers on microfilm organized by Kuhlman in 1935 (38). Bendikson (270), in a paper published in 1935, maintained that reproductions on 35 millimeter film if carefully made and preserved would have a long life. Bits of Dagron's films made during the siege of Paris which were still in good condition constituted the chief basis for his claim.

Tests then being made at the National Bureau of Standards and nitrate film and cellulose acetate film were briefly described by Scribner (328) who stated, among other things:

> While the evidence is not yet complete, that already obtained shows that acetate films offer considerable promise for permanent record use if properly made and if care is taken to prevent them from drying out too much.

Hill and Weber (329) in a paper based on National Bureau of Standards studies described the methods of tests of cellulose acetate and cellulose nitrate film and the results. They stated:

> In all tests the acetate type showed much greater resistence to deterioration than did the nitrate film. The results indicate that acetate film is a very stable material, being comparable to permanent record paper in its resistance to accelerated aging. The nitrate type of film was found to be comparatively unstable.

Physical properties studied were folding endurance and loss of weight; chemical properties were acidity, stability, copper number, viscosity, and the effects of aging upon gelatin emulsion.

National Bureau of Standards tests were explicitly described in another paper by Hill and Weber (330). These authors included specific recommendations on the properties of cellulose acetate film for the preservation of records of permanent value as follows:

1. A folding endurance of not less than 16 single folds, with not less than 75 per cent retention of folding endurance after heating 72 hours at 100°C.
2. A pH value of not less than 5.5, with a decrease of not more than 0.5 after heating 72 hours at 100°C.
3. An increase in copper number after heating 72 hours at 100°C. of not more than 0.2.
4. A decrease in relative viscosity after heating 72 hours at 100°C. of not more than 3.0 per cent.
5. Developed film shall be free from sodium thiosulphate (hypo) as indicated by the mercuric chloride test, and the base should be free from cellulose nitrate as indicated by the diphenylamine test.

Kimberley and Scribner (331) stated (p. 26) that when the National Bureau of Standards undertook its investigations of nitrate and cellulose films, there was practically no authoritative information available on their stability or how they should be used and stored. They summarized the reactions of these two classes of film to accelerated aging tests and to tests designed to determine chemical deterioration and mentioned that effect of the light of projectors, of contaminated air and the resistance of photographic emulsion to aging and to wear were still to be investigated.

In a less formal paper, Scribner (332) stressed the importance of the specifications for stable film quoted in the second paragraph above and advised against buying film for permanent records by the generic name "acetate film" or by brand name alone, since acetate film as generally made does not always meet these standards of quality. He stated that acetate film of the usual commercial grade was probably suitable for reading room use since films which are used will become unserviceable through scratching and other wear and tear; but that negative film preserved as the permanent record and used only for making positive prints should comply with the recommended specifications. He referred to the Bureau's recognition of the need for four classes of record papers to preserve records: 1. indefinitely, 2. for 50 to 100 years, 3. for 25 to 50 years, 4. about 5 years, and indicated that a parallel classification of film for record purposes was desirable.

In a paper given at a congress of industrial chemists, Clement and Riviere reported the effects of aging on celluloid, nitrocellulose and cellulose acetate. Instead of applying accelerated aging techniques to fresh samples, they studied samples known to be twenty-five years old. Furthermore, their samples had been gathered from several commercial sources. They studied both powders and films. In general, their results--which are presented in detail--indicated greater chemical and mechanical stability in these materials than had been indicated by the National Bureau of Standards accelerated aging tests. They concluded that acetate film is a stable material, suitable for the preservation of precious documents.

Scribner (334) reported on the findings made in approximately four years of research at the National Bureau of Standards on the life expectancy of microfilm. Nitrate base and acetate base motion picture type films in which the image is formed in an emulsion and viscose base and acetate base dye-impregnated films of the Ozaphane type were studied. Experimental techniques of accelerated aging figured largely in the tests made. Results indicated that cellulose acetate film meeting stated specifications is a very stable material and that micro-images on it have a high degree of permanency if washed free of processing chemicals, especially hypo. On the other hand, nitrate film was found too unstable for permanent records and the tests indicated that the viscose film had a durability approximately equal to papers made from a medium grade of bleached wood fibers. The tests covered not only stability, but also chemical purity and mechanical strength.

National Bureau of Standards research eventually culminated in the publication of a standard for permanent record microfilm (335) which set up exact specifications for the emulsion, processing, hypo content, flexibility, composition of film base, relative viscosity, pH stability, nitrogen content, and provided explicit descriptions of test procedures.

A broad discussion of the stability of microfilm was incorporated in a paper by Würstlin (336) who pointed out that the durability of the base film depends upon its chemical composition, that the manufacture of film is a highly technical procedure during which the product is tested for quality. As first made, cellulose acetate film was not a suitable material for permanent microcopy, but it was later improved. The fixing and washing of exposed film are important factors in its permanency. The author recommended that the fixing time be twice as long as usual and that the fixing chemicals should be changed frequently. The film should be washed in a rapidly flowing bath and should be tested for hypo concentration. Storage requirements for permanency are also discussed.

The technical characteristics of microfilm which are factors in its durability were explained in a non-technical style by Offenhauser (217). He pointed out that the film consists of an emulsion .001 inch thick on a base .005 inch thick. Aging of the base is discussed and the author expresses the opinion that the deterioration rate of film base then in use in microfilm was significantly slower than the most durable grades of paper commercially available. However, he noted that a specific description of permanence would have to begin with a specification of chemical composition and this varies from manufacturer to manufacturer. He shows that the principle ingredient of the emulsion is gelatin, an organic material subject to fungal and bacterial attack. A temperature of 85°F. and relative humidity of 85 per cent or fluctuating temperatures under conditions that cause condensation of moisture are noted as favorable conditions for biological attack on the gelatin.

Standards and terminology. Approved standards such as those of the American Standards Association pertinent to microcopying contain outstanding descriptions of quality factors in both finished microcopies and in materials and equipment used in production of microcopies. In addition, they also contain approved definitions of terms and describe approved procedures for tests. Nevertheless, the standards literature will not be covered in detail in this report. One reason is that a mere list of applicable standards, including those of the United States of America, Great Britain and Germany, would easily number several hundred titles. Furthermore, the typical standard is a concisely expressed document which cannot be condensed without omitting essential information. The development of standards in microcopying will be traced and a selection of the important standards will be mentioned.

In terminology a somewhat different situation exists. Problems in terminology develop practically abreast with any given field of science or technology. In microcopying discussions of terms and short glossaries began to appear early, but their usefulness was lost in most cases as soon as better and more authoritative lists appeared. Therefore, only a few of the more significant discussions and lists will be mentioned.

As early as 1935 a Committee of Library Experts working under the auspices of the International Office of Chemistry made recommendations (337) on standards and terminology. They recommended adoption of 35 mm. film with a width of 24 mm. for the image and spelled out other specifications regarding size. They recommended adoption of the following terms and definitions:

Microphotographie: photographie à l'aide d'un microscope. Image obtenu par ce procédé et representant l'objet en proportions fortement grossies.
Microphotocopie: copie d'une document, obtenu par la procédé microphotographique.
Photomicrographie: photographie à l'aide d'un dispositif optique réduisant fortement les proportions de l'objet à photographier. Image obtenu par ce procédé et ne pouvant être lue qu'a l'aide d'uns appareil grossisant.
Photomicrocopie: copie d'une document, obtenu par un procédé photomicrographique.
Photomicrofilm et par extension microfilm: microphotocopie par film.

In a paper published in 1936 Metcalf (46) pointed to the lack of standards as one of the things holding back development in microcopying. He mentioned that a standardization committee of the National Research Council had been formed and was at work on the problems of standardization requiring experimentation and study. In the same year the National

Bureau of Standards (338) published a simplified practice recommendation in which two film widths, 16 mm. and 35 mm. were recommended for record copying.

Clapp wrote at length about the things in need of standardization, such as film width, frame size, film thickness, image position, and reduction ratio, but in the same article made a strong plea for more experimentation before the adoption of rigid standards. Sayce and others in two papers (249, 316) urged rigid standardization while library use of microphotography was still young. They discussed various features of microfilm in need of standardization, but assumed that standard double-perforated film would be used because so much work had been done on such film, because the perforated edges provided a safe area for handling, and because so many cameras in use were built for it. They made five recommendations covering film widths, perforation, film base, dimensions of image, position of image, size of screen in the reader, and length of film strips.

Standardization on an international basis was discussed at the 15th Conference of the International Federation for Documentation. Tate (339), in an informal report on the Conference named the participants in the discussion on standardization and described the proposals. The latter included the use of reduction ratios not greater than 12:1 and 35 mm. double perforate film to facilitate international exchange and interlibrary loan. Maximum size of the image on the film, order and placement of the images and nomenclature of the placements also were discussed.

Bobb (340), after stating (p. 325): "Under no circumstances should standardization be permitted to freeze the development of microphotography, especially at this early stage," went on to point out that standards, presumably tentative, were needed so that microfilm purchasers could be certain that microfilm received was of high quality. He discussed standards under the subheads "Film testing," "Reading machines," "Film storage and handling," "Standard format" and "Cataloging microfilm," referring to National Bureau of Standards tests and recommendations on points where these applied such as temperature and humidity requirements in storage; but on other points he described good practices instead of stating specific standards.

The American Standards Association published an American Standard (341) for permanent record film in 1945, and another standard (342) covering microfilming in 1947. The latter contained an approved definition of the term "microfilm" and specifications for the film base, width, format, image placement, etc. The British Standards Institution (343) issued specifications for microfilm readers and microfilm in 1947.

A Committee on the Photographic Reproduction of Research Materials of the Association of Research Libraries (344) published in 1950 a proposed standard for the microcopying of newspapers. This document covered definitions of basic terms, materials, bibliographical treatment, film identification and arrangement, procedures for incomplete and damaged files, camera adjustments and other points of photographic techniques, and assembly and filing of completed films. In 1951 Rider (121) made a plea for the adoption as standard the size 7-1/2 x 12-1/2 cm. for microtexts, whether on opaque or transparent materials.

At the 18th International Conference of the Federation for Documentation (345), the use of the terms "a. microcopy; b. microfilm; c. microfiches; d. microcard" with "microfiches" reserved for sheet microfilm and "microcard" for opaque cards was recommended. The recommendations were made in the light of the work of Technical Committee 46 of the International Standards Organization. It was also recommended that the Council of the International Federation for Documentation prepare and submit to Unesco "a plan for study and research in the format and dimension of microcopies with a view to standardization..." In a report of the first meeting of Sub-Committee I of Technical Committee 46 of the International Organization for Standardization (346), "two draft recommendations, No. X, Microcopies and No. Y, Terminology of Photographic and Light Copying Processes, were discussed."

An announcement (347) was published of the formation of a new committee (later designated as PH5 of the American Standards Association) to work on "...standards for photographic materials, apparatus and processes pertaining to production, use, storage and preservation of document reproductions." Three subcommittees were set up to cover 1. microfilm and other microtransparencies, 2. microopaques, including microcards and microprint, and 3. documents readable without optical devices. One of the Committee's announced functions was to present the American point of view in related work of the International Organization for Standardization.

Clapp (348) discussed very briefly the status of standards in photographic reproduction of documents. He mentioned the efforts of Subcommittee 1 of Technical Committee 46, Standards in Library Work and Documentation, of the International Standards Organization and of Unesco and gave an account of the beginnings of Committee PH5 of the American Standards Association which was organized in response to needs for more precise standards for microfilm and for United States of America participation in the activities of the International Standards Organization in the same field.

A much fuller discussion of the status of international standardization was written by Frontard (349) who described the activities of the International Organization for Standardization, particularly this organization's Technical Documentation Committee and its Documentary Reproduction Sub-Committee. The importance of ISO's influence on standardization of documentary microcopying on a national basis was brought out, and the status of the problems before it on terminology, classification and dimensions of bases, standardization of the various forms of microfilm, and of microsheets and microcards was discussed.

Publication of a glossary of microfilm terms sponsored by the National Microfilm Association's Committee on Terminology has been noted (135, 136). Duyvis (350) presented a broad view of standardization, considering both macroscopic and microscopic copying. He stated that it seemed desirable to adhere to the width of moving picture film, using the area between perforations for the images, and referred to several American, British, and German standards where this dimension is upheld. He listed as standard sizes for microcards and microsheets 75 x 125 mm., 74 x 105 mm. and 9 x 12 cm.

Martijn (351) discussed the necessity of cooperation in order to solve problems of format and storage of microfilm. He stated that the standard length in Belgium was 10 or 30 meters although few books require more than two meters of film. The provisional International Organization for Standardization micro test object is described and illustrated. A provisional terminology of microcopies and their bases giving the definitions in English and French of the following terms is included: "Microcopy," "Scale," "Roll microfilm," "Strip microfilm (or micro-strip?)" "Micro-sheet or microfilm sheet," "Roll microcopy on paper," "Strip microcopy on paper" and "Micro-card."

A manual (138) of good microfilming practices compiled by the American Library Association's Committee on Photoduplication and Multiple Copying Methods was in large part a systematized presentation of American Standards Association standards. However, in areas not covered by these standards, it described "norms" or good practices in an effort to make a comprehensive guide for microfilm laboratories as an aid in the standardization of permanent record microfilm. All of the common aspects of production of permanent record microfilm, including definitions, photographic materials, types of material microfilmed, bibliographical treatment of newspapers, books, pamphlets, serials, manuscripts and maps, procedures in cases of damaged and incomplete examples or files, etc., are covered.

Studies (352) in progress by the American Standards Association Committee PH5 in late 1955 were described. Standardization of microcopying was the subject of a special number of the journal Courrier de normalisation (353). The over-all viewpoint was international, but there was some emphasis on French standards, French activities in standardization, and French apparatus and materials.

Standardization activities in the United States of America, in European countries, and internationally were described by Holmes (354). The structure, activities and procedures of the American Standards Association were explained, and the organization of its Committee PH5 was stated in detail. Also discussed were the standardization activities of the Association of Research Libraries and the American Library Association. The latter's Guide to microfilming practices (138) and its relations to American Standards Association standards were discussed. Activities of the Library of Congress in regard to microfilming standards and tests were described. The meeting during the previous summer of the International Organization for Standardization was briefly reviewed and the activities of its committees on photographic matters were outlined. Twelve items on which action was taken at the meeting were listed.

Numerous American Standards Association standards and some other standards are listed in the text and bibliographies, and several standards are reproduced in full in the appendix of Lewis and Offenhauser's book (143). Many of the standards listed or quoted apply to photographic materials or methods rather than to microphotography. However, all of the important American standards approved or proposed in the field of microcopying when this book was written are listed at one place or another in it.

Production Costs

A search of the literature can only lead to the conclusion that there is very little information published on the costs of producing documentary microcopies. Information is readily available on charges made by libraries and others for supplying microcopies to scholars and other institutions, but it is doubtful if these charges, at least in most cases, are based on production costs. Most of the useful published information on costs deals with factors in costs rather than the over-all picture. This literature, or at least a part of it, could serve as groundwork for a thorough study of production costs.

The cost data in Binkley's first publication on the reproduction of research materials (16) are limited largely to materials costs and, of course, are based on manufacturers' charges at the time that book was written. On pages 83-84 Binkley points out that photostat paper for a full size reproduction of a 50-page issue of the New York Times would cost $86, but that a 24:1 reduction of the same material could be copied on 3 cents worth of film.

In 1932, a paper by Henry (18) contained (p. 216) the following information on contemporary costs:

> ...the Library of Congress is finding that with Lemare equipment they can produce films at a cost of about one and one half cents per page. Harvard, with Leica equipment, is producing films at an even lower cost. But these do not include general overhead, so commercial prices quoted are somewhat higher. The published prices of the French firm (Société des Editions sur Films des Bibliothèques Nationales de France) mentioned above average about 6 cents per page.

In an article published the following year, Henry (23) gave the prices then being charged by the libraries of Harvard University, Yale University, the Library of Congress and the Henry E. Huntington Library and Art Gallery for microfilm copies and (in some cases) enlargements from microfilms. Charges ranged from 1-1/2 cents to 5 cents per page. In the same article it is stated that the Filmograph Corporation whose chief business had been copying long files of public records was quoting a rate of 2 cents per page on orders of 100,000 pages or more of bound volumes and would reproduce a file of the London Times running to about a million pages for 1-1/2 cents per page.

Bendikson (270), while advocating reduced copies on paper, did point out that the material cost of film reproductions is less, but that if it is necessary to enlarge the images in order to use them, the cost of paper for the enlargements would equal the cost of photostat paper. Seidell (39) estimated in a paper published in 1935 that the film used for a microcopy for a ten-page article would cost about 2 cents and that developing and labor about 8 cents, making the cost "...10 cents per article of 10 pages or less and 5 cents for each additional 10 pages."

In an analysis (355) of the first seven months' operation of the Bibliofilm Service, it was stated that:

> The records of cost...indicate that the rates specified, namely, ten cents for each article not exceeding ten pages in length, and five cents for each additional page or fraction thereof, of the same article, are sufficient to cover the actual cost of the film, the time of taking the photographs, the chemicals, and the work of developing the films. ...they have not covered the cost of keeping the records and the correspondence. ... clerical costs are no greater than those connected with the lending of books.... It was never intended that the cost of looking up the references or getting the books from the shelves should be added to the cost of the film copies, as no charge would be made for the service if the person requesting the reference visited the Library in person.

Schellenberg (356) in a paper published in 1935 estimated (p. 291) that 3,200 pages of the Congressional record could be reproduced on 16 mm. film at a film cost of $5.50 with a rented commercial Recordak. Binkley (p. 4 of reference 162) presented an analysis of the factors in cost of making single microcopies. He mentioned materials costs, labor costs, and camera features. Labor cost, although incurred only once, varies according to the conditions of the project and may include so much "traveling about, so much collating and arranging that the actual costs of manipulation of the camera is only a fraction of the total labor cost..." High labor costs are associated with copying short runs such as 10, 20, or 30 pages. Camera features affecting costs include the optical system which governs the degree of reduction possible, provision (or lack of it) for adjusting the area of film exposed at one exposure and the length of film accommodated since long rolls allow continuous processing.

A panel of librarians (64) surveying the state of microcopying failed in 1936 to discover any library that had kept a separate account of the costs of processing microfilm and could do no better on the cost problem than to cite contemporary charges of libraries to patrons. The same panel mentioned that frame-by-frame inspection could cost more than the whole remainder of the production of microcopies. Metcalf (46) included a brief analysis of cost factors in a paper published in 1936. He pointed out (p. 12) that making short runs on individual order would always be expensive because of the clerical overhead costs and that the advantage of lower material costs for microfilm as compared to photostat would be lost unless a means could be found for reducing these overhead expenses. His proposed solution to the cost problem was a central organization which would maintain a large file of master negatives from which prints could be made at low cost, thus avoiding the costs of assembling documents to fill individual orders and making it possible to use automatic machinery in making prints and enlargements.

In an account of the activities of Science Service toward the development of microcopying, Davis (44) stated that Bibliofilm Service was then making microfilm copies at a cost to the user of about a cent a page, and 6" x 8" enlarged prints from microfilm negatives at about 5 cents a page.

Binkley's Manual (45) contains a wide range of information on costs. Costs are discussed under the following subheads (p. 125):

> Cost of Photosensitive Surface. Film on Glass Versus Paper. Film, Glass or Paper? Film Strips or Rectangles? Full Use of Area of Moving Picture Film. Processing Costs. First Costs and Running Costs in Microcopying. Microcopying (Reprint Costs). Short Footages in Unique Copies.

Tables pertaining to costs and entitled as follows are included: p. 126, "Price per square foot of usable surface;" p. 127, "Comparative prices of photographic surface on paper, glass, and film; with reduction ratios to bring prices to common levels; Figures for 256 square feet of pages reduced photographically by the following reduction ratios: 6, 8, 11, 16, 22-1/2;" p. 129, "Film footages required in copying books in different positions on 35 mm. film (perforated on both sides) and 16 mm. film, using full width of film; Prices of film processing;" p. 130, "Effect of variation of processing costs on price of microcopy positive of a book of 100 pages, 6" x 9", in varying reduction ratios (16 mm. film calculated at .43" width of usable surface)."

Binkley pointed out (p. 115) that there is a constant temptation in microcopying to reproduce as large a number of words as possible on a given area of film in order to reduce material costs and cited "the mathematical law that utilization of area increases by squares while reduction of linear dimension of the writing proceeds arithmetically." He distinguished (p. 31) between first costs and running costs. The first cost is the cost of the negative; the running cost is the cost of each additional positive print.

Binkley cited the experiences of the Filmograph Corporation, Lloyd B. Kennedy and the Recordak Corporation in microcopying large volumes of uniform-sized material to support an estimate that in copying such material one operator can photograph 10,000 pages per day. He stated that labor cost is independent of reduction ratio and hence of the amount of film used. However, assuming $10 per day wages for two operators, a reduction ratio of 16 to 23 diameters, and processing costs obtainable with long runs, he estimated that $10 worth of labor will photograph $12 to $15 worth of film, including processing.

Turning to the making of short footages of microfilm in unique copies, Binkley stated (p. 134):

> If the number of pages to be copied per day in a library should be large enough to allow the continuous operation of the machine, the operating cost would rise above that of a long run of uniform materials only to the extent that readjustments of forms become necessary in changing from books of one page size to books of another size. The processing costs could still stand at the level of long run work. An additional charge would

be incurred in cutting up the strips and mailing the short lengths to various purchasers, but this type of service, in the experience of the Recordak Corporation would not lift the costs to an entirely new level. Bookkeeping costs would appear, but it seems quite probable that on large-scale work the price level could be held down within striking distance of the price of long footage orders.

In an article based on the rather extensive photocopying experience of Armstrong College Library, Patterson (47) pointed out (p. 349) the lower cost of materials and processing for microfilm as compared to glass negatives and estimated that in a library making full use of a microcopying camera, savings were as much as three-fourths of the cost of older methods. Carruthers (43) analyzed the cost of microfilming in comparison to photostats and photographic prints on 70 mm. paper. He found a cost advantage in microfilm for long runs, but pointed out that microfilm copying of short runs lacked this advantage because of the lower speed of operation and overhead expenses. He stressed the importance of administrative expenses and stated that in photoprinting services these were equal to processing costs. He went on to say that it was doubtful whether microfilm copies could be supplied for much less than 5 cents a page for short runs and pointed out that 5 cents a page would also be the cost of copies on 70 mm. paper at much lower reduction ratios. In a discussion of reduced scale prints on photostat paper, Binkley (45) pointed out (p. 119) that material costs tended to dictate high reduction ratios even on paper because if paper copies were made from film negatives, the costs of the paper would be a predominant factor.

Metcalf (357), in a paper urging that the development of microphotography in libraries be directed by a central organization, included considerable information on contemporary costs, but supplied no evidence in support of his figures. Champlin (302) gave the cost in dollars of two editions of volumes containing theses reproduced in miniature by a lithoprinting process. In one instance, an edition of 600 copies of an 80-page volume costs $107. In the other, 800 copies of a 274-page volume cost $115. No breakdown of the factors in these costs was given. Bendikson (73) estimated that microfilm negatives and positive prints on paper made from the negatives could be produced for a total cost of 6 cents per book opening or 3 cents per page. Apparently, however, the figures were a guess, for he stated that they were in all probability too high.

Hypothetical costs for the microcopying of 10 million pages of text in a cooperative venture shared by ten libraries were presented by Binkley (71). He pointed out in the same article that the lowest unit in microcopying is obtained when a long run of pages is copied uniformly and in sequence, while at the other extreme is the making of microcopies of books and periodical articles in lieu of interlibrary loans. In connection with the latter, he mentioned that the administrative cost of organizing a collection of microcopies of short runs would exceed the cost of recopying the material for each user.

In an important survey (182) of the status of microphotography published in 1938, it was pointed out that little attention had been given to cost accounting for two reasons: 1. the inexpensiveness of the process, and 2. the many variable factors and alternative procedures. On p. 54, these factors were outlined as follows: 1. variation in nature and format of originals and in the kinds of copies which can be made from them. 2. The kind of film and processing required. 3. The ratio of reduction in terms of probable use. 4. The number of pages to be copied and the number of copies desired. 5. Overhead, including personnel, equipment, obsolescence. 6. Copying in the field or in a laboratory. 7. The cost of servicing originals to the camera. These factors are further discussed. For example, it is explained that 7. includes the costs of correspondence, accounting, delivering, and reshelving. Some factors in the costs of microcopying books, manuscripts, and archival materials were discussed by Jenkinson and Sayce (230). These authors stated that between 1,000 and 2,000 pages of a book can be copied in an hour after the book has been positioned and the camera adjusted. On the other hand, manuscripts and archives present difficult and varying photographic problems. Each exposure must be considered individually and in some cases a number of experimental exposures must be made; in archival material there is often considerable variation in the sizes of successive documents, often there is difficulty in mounting material beneath the camera so that it will be held flat and at the same time prevent damage to the document or its binding. The authors reached the conclusion that it will never be possible to standardize prices for the microcopying of archives.

In a paper read at an international conference, Binkley (358) compared the costs of printing from type, blueprinting, diazo printing, and microfilm, according to the number of copies required. Rates charged in 1938 for microfilm copies by Bibliofilm Service (359), University of Chicago (360), and the University of Michigan (361) were published. None of the notices indicated that the rates had been based on a study of production costs.

Cost factors in the microcopying at a high-quality level of long runs of material were discussed by Case (306). He stated that the highest element of cost is apt to be faulty work which must be done over. He placed the most emphasis upon the camera which if manufactured to do high quality work would have automatic features. These would save operators' time and reduce waste of film and time. He stated that since the cost of developing, fixing, washing and drying is only about one-tenth of the total cost of processing, high speed, mass production developing machinery such as is used by the motion picture industry could reduce the total cost only about 3 per cent.

Various factors in microcopying costs were brought out in a comparison (362) of the methods and fees of several Washington, D. C. agencies, including Bibliofilm Service and Medicofilm Service. Bookkeeping was noted as one of the largest factors in cost. To avoid it Medicofilm Service adopted the practice of indicating the amount due on the customer's order blank and returning it with the completed microfilm, the bill to be paid by the customer after receiving the microfilm. Bibliofilm Service did not include in its costs the expense of bringing books to the microfilm camera even though this cost had been estimated at about 25 cents per hour.

The average cost of correspondence, clerical work, bringing the book to the camera, etc. was 50 cents in one library, but the customer was charged only 25 cents. (The text does not make it clear whether 25 cents was a total or minimum charge per order, or whether a service charge of 25 cents was made.) A representative of the Library of Congress noted that as the organization of the microcopying service became complex, prices naturally rose. It was indicated that vague descriptions of items wanted and requests in foreign languages were factors in costs at the Library of Congress.

Microcopying costs in India were given in rather general terms and in the currency of that nation by Trivedi (363).

In two papers published in 1941 Seidell discussed microcopying costs. In the first one (89) he debated whether readers should be charged at all for microfilm copying in view of the fact that they are not charged for services rendered when using libraries in person. He then made the suggestion that publicly supported reference libraries should perform microfilm copying as freely as they lend books or provide facilities for consulting them.

In the second article, Seidell (364) discussed costs of microfilm copying in some detail. He ruled out cost or amortization of microfilm equipment on the grounds that interest on the capital invested in libraries and their furnishings is not considered a part of their operating expenses. Furthermore, he did not consider the cost of keeping and collecting accounts since this would not be necessary if the service was operated without charge to the users of microcopies. With these factors of expense eliminated, he then analyzed the costs of filling orders for 100 different articles in 100 different bound or unbound periodicals. Film and developing chemicals for the 100 microfilms were estimated at $1.75. On the basis of experience in the Army Medical Library, he estimated that two hours would be needed to find and bring 100 books to the camera and one hour would be needed to replace them on the shelves.

The operations of loading the camera, placing the book, adjusting the focus, turning the pages and removing the book was estimated at four hours for 100 volumes. Developing, fixing, etc. for 120 feet of film was estimated at one and one half hours. Comparing the film copy with the original, cutting the film into strips, and attaching the strips to the order blanks was estimated on the basis of experience at three hours. Placing the 100 microfilms in envelopes or boxes and addressing them for mailing was estimated at four hours for 100 orders. Wages were figured at $1 per hour and the total cost of making the 100 microfilms was shown to be $17.25, which the author designated as a liberal estimate subject to reduction as organization of the work improved.

Practical difficulties which affect costs of microfilming of newspapers and other documents were discussed by Worth (365). These included discoloration of pages, changes in page size, and brittleness of paper making rapid turning of pages impossible. The author felt that such factors required a downward revision of production rates as given in the literature and a more factual approach to estimating costs.

A time and cost study of the Bibliofilm Service of the United States Department of Agriculture Library was presented by Shaw (366). A flow chart of the operations of the Service shows a division of the cost elements into three groups: 1. cost of connected library service; 2. business office costs; 3. materials and labor in the microfilm laboratory. The author pointed out that different weights would be given to these components by other institutions and that costs in library laboratories and commercial laboratories could not be compared because 1. commercial firms do not do reference work or get the publications to be copied from library shelves and 2. library laboratories rarely have the overhead costs of commercial laboratories.

Each cost component is discussed in the light of Bibliofilm Service experience and special studies of its operations. For example, it is stated that no charge was made against the cost of providing photocopies for normal library operations such as getting books from the shelves and returning them to the shelves, since these things were done without charge for readers who visited the library or sought information by letter or telephone. Office costs are stated to include costs of correspondence, handling and accounting for funds, editing and mailing of the photocopies. A breakdown of the Service's office costs into these elements during a two-month period when 1,207 items were supplied is given in a table. However, in another table covering the office costs of a shorter period when 757 items were supplied, the breakdown among the three elements came out different, although the total cost per item supplied was the same.

It is noted that materials and laboratory labor costs include the film, the photographing, developing, drying, etc. Depreciation and obsolescence of equipment was not accounted for although the author noted that this is a factor in total costs. A breakdown of laboratory time in hours among the activities of filming, administration of the laboratory, care of equipment and preparation of solutions, and developing is presented for a period of four weeks during which 60,007 frames of film were produced. These times were converted into costs at the wage rates paid, and the figures were broken down by activity and given in a table. Total costs divided among laboratory labor materials, office costs and other charges were given. The net result was a cost per frame of 1.71 cents.

Special factors in the Service's costs such as the purchasing of film and paper under federal contracts and higher salaries are mentioned. It was noted also that office costs are 80 per cent of total cost of copying periodical articles and 30 per cent of the total cost for all the work handled. Some of the office costs were due to non-productive activities such as telling customers that material could not be supplied and making refunds.

In a general treatise on library photographic reproduction, Fussler (198) discussed (chapter II) the principles of computing costs of operations and (chapter IX) the elements of costs and rates for microfilming. On page 184 he pointed out that adequacy and completeness of the equipment and personnel and the volume and type of work affect the costs of microfilming. Since these factors vary from institution to institution, fixed ratios among them are not possible. Furthermore, in large laboratories with fully mechanized equipment, unit costs will be smaller than in small laboratories. The cost of copying rare and fragile materials is higher (p. 185) than the cost of copying current printed materials. Cost studies have limited applications because of variations in service and amounts of work, types of reproduction and quality, and form of the finished product. The necessity for minimum charges is discussed at some length, and the contemporary rates for microfilming of the Library of Congress and the University of Chicago are compared. The April, 1941 rates of 14 libraries supplying microfilm are presented in a table on p. 188. An account begins on p. 189 of records kept by the microfilming laboratory of the University of Chicago. Although these records presumably could be used to determine times and labor costs, no information is included on man hours and actual production costs.

Shaw (367) discussed the results of studies of the cost of producing microfilm and the cost of producing photoprints. The photoprints were made on semiautomatic equipment and by enlargement from film (p. 738). Significant differences were found only in direct labor and materials costs. Although the sensitized paper used for the photoprints cost less than one-tenth as much as film per unit area, material costs were considerably higher for photoprints because of the larger areas used. Labor costs were higher for the photoprints for each stage of the operation except editing. However, costs for checking and mailing film were so much greater than for the same operations in photoprints that continuous strip photoprints of average articles cost less to produce (p. 741).

Production costs of microcards were discussed tentatively and apparently without much analysis on p. 117 and elsewhere in Rider's The scholar and the future of the research library (274). Rider's estimates were questioned by Metcalf in a symposium (275) based on The scholar.... Metcalf asked (p. 172) whether adequate weight had been given to administrative costs when a selling price of 5 cents per card was suggested and pointed out that publishers had found that overhead costs do not increase with production costs. In a reply to the question, Rider (p. 181) admitted that the price of 5 cents a card was very tentative and pointed to his suggestions that first cards should cost more than succeeding ones and that cards sold individually should cost more than those bought in lots. He reasserted that the price of 5 cents each would prove to be enough for cards issued in large editions.

In an effort to establish a basis for sound estimates of the cost of documentary reproduction, including photostat, microfilm, hectograph and mimeograph, Janicki (368) collected information from a number of sources, including the American Institute of Documentation, the U. S. Department of Agriculture library, the British Museum, and the State Library in Berlin. Although the author recognized that it is difficult to make exact cost calculations or even close estimates because of the varied work and conditions, he offered two formulas, supplied to him by the Schweizerische Lichtbildanstalt:

The English Formula

Cost of material	20%
Cost of labour (Salaries, Wages)	40%
Overhead (General) Charges	20%
Net profit	20%

The Swiss Formula

Cost of Material	10%
Cost of Labour (Salaries, Wages)	35%
Overhead (General) Charges	35%
Net profit	20%

As given above the formulas are for application by profit-making firms. To adapt them for non-profit-making institutions, the percentage indicated for "Net profit" is allocated evenly to the other three factors.

From these formulas Janicki derived an "average formula" for profit-making enterprises and another one for non-profit-making institutions. The latter reads as follows:

Cost of Material	18-1/2%
Cost of Labour (Salaries, Wages)	47%
General (Overhead) Charges	34-1/2%

In applying these formulas materials cost is suggested as a starting point, but any other factor may be used instead.

Janicki stated that on the basis of detail supplied by the Dutch Institute of Documentation, correlated with information from other sources and taking actual salaries into account, satisfactory estimates of working costs for photocopying in libraries could be made. However, he did not give these details, show the correlation, or give an illustrative estimate other than the above quoted average formula. He did say that in the cases of libraries with photographic departments it was assumed that the book collecting service would be available to these departments without charge.

Among the miscellaneous information included in Janicki's article: when copying on rolls of 35 mm. film accommodating from 825 to 1,000 exposures, the man-hour requirement is 20 minutes per order, or 21 orders per seven-hour day (an unpublished memorandum by S. C. Bradford is given credit for this figure). It is stated that the State Library of Berlin reckons 15 minutes per order, or 28 orders per 7-1/2-hour day. Supervision costs are given in terms of money. Charges to consumers rather than production costs are given for a number of leading institutions.

Information on cost estimates of microfilming was published in a War Department Technical manual (105). However, since the basis of the estimates was a file drawer or cabinet or records, the data given are not applicable to many library microfilming projects. It is stated (p. 13) that experience of the War Department indicates that on the average project a camera operator can photograph 1-1/2 drawers of records per day and that an additional 1/2 man-day is required for inspection and indexing of the film and that one additional person is required on the job to prepare the papers for the camera by removing staples, etc. The total man-days for microfilming the contents of a four-drawer cabinet was estimated at 6.65. Some data are given also on the photographing of card records and a project is mentioned in which the operator averaged three drawers of records per day. Total labor costs and film costs based on the use of 16 mm. film for microfilming four-drawer cabinets of records are estimated, but no estimate is furnished for cost of microfilming with a flat-bed camera using 35 mm. film. Instead it is stated that such costs and production rates vary widely.

Edwards (303) provided information on the costs in terms of cents per page of offset printing in miniature for five rates of reduction and for small editions of several sizes ranging from ten copies to 100 copies. No information was given on whether the figures quoted included the firm's overhead and profit, and, of course, there was no breakdown into labor and materials. In an analysis of factors in the cost of microfilm, Power (251) pointed out that the cost of the negative is the highest and that after it is produced, positive copies may be printed off at a declining cost up to ten copies, after which the cost remains constant regardless of the number produced. Numerous factors, such as operator experience, were, in his opinion, difficult to measure. However, he listed and discussed six tangible factors as follows: 1. the efficiency and ease of the camera operation. 2. the width and quality of the film. 3. the position of the image. 4. processing, printing, and handling procedure. 5. the laboratory's standards. 6. roll versus strip microfilm. Power stressed that the major cost in microfilming is labor rather than material, nevertheless the figures he gave are in dollars, not man-hours.

Addressing the Medical Library Association, Rider (327, p. 13) said that microcards are cheaper than microfilm if more than five copies are required, and gave a figure of $15 for a microcard edition of 100 copies of a work containing 100 pages. Meeuwis (370) published cost comparisons of a number of copying processes including typewriting, printing, mimeographing, photocopy and microcopy. Actual costs of production were quoted in guilders only. Power (117) in a paper on the substitution of microfilm for bound copies of periodicals in libraries compared costs of 16 mm. film with 35 mm. film and showed that little would be saved by 16 mm. Also he saw little economy in substituting paper for film in microcopying because the higher cost of the film is offset by the economies of producing microfilm in long length (p. 141).

Some information on production costs of microfiche or

transparent microcards is given by van der Wolk and Tonnon (119). They assume manufacture on a commercial basis and furnish a chart showing prices in various currencies for microfiches containing various numbers of images. Analyses are presented of the costs of reproducing a 208-page book and a periodical article. Neither analysis discusses cost factors other than number of copies made. It is shown, for example, that when the book is copied at a reduction of 1:17 and five sets of microfiches are made, the cost per set is less than one-third the cost of the original book. Costs of transforming indexes and indexed material into "one-copy microcards" by pasting film strips to card stock were discussed by Rider (288). A comparison of this form of microcopy with conventional microfilm is implied, and the author points out that the photographing which must be done for either form is the largest single item of cost. The costs noted are low, but it is indicated they are based on the work being done by inexpensive labor. All estimates are in terms of money rather than man-hours.

Kuipers (290) in an article on the implications of microcards for documentation stated that microcards could be supplied to the document user at a fraction of the current microcard price. He appeared to base this contention on the economies that would be achieved when specialized equipment with automatic and continuous features was made available. He pointed out that photofinishers using continuous processing and automatic printers made ten snapshot prints for the price of one microcard. However, he indicated that microcard costs would always be higher because of more expensive sensitized materials and additional operations.

Power (371) disputed a prevalent notion that microfilm was the least expensive microcopying process for one to fifteen copies, while other methods were cheaper if more than fifteen copies were needed. He stated that in quantities of 30 or 100 or 400 microfilm could be produced for one-third cent to one-sixth cent per page. He compared costs of microcopying a 300-page document by the microfilm process and by offset lithography and showed that an addition of 100 microfilm copies would cost substantially less per copy than the cost per copy of an edition of 100 produced by offset lithography or even an edition of 500 produced by the same process. The article contains no breakdown of costs and no information on relative times for the two processes.

A number of factors that influence the cost of making microfilm were mentioned in a paper (372) devoted primarily to the comparative costs of storing original documents and microfilm copies of them. Among the factors mentioned were: type of camera (that is, whether a high-speed continuous flow camera capable of copying only single sheets may be used or whether the nature of the material requires the use of automatic or table camera such as are used for copying from books); whether the material requires infolding; whether it requires a heavy sheet of glass to hold it down under the camera; whether fading or coloring necessitates the use of panchromatic film, filters, or longer exposures; whether it requires careful handling because of fragility or other reason. Most of the data on costs given in this paper pertain to storage and maintenance and are referred to elsewhere in this report.

The elements of cost in producing microfiches with Microlex cameras were discussed at length by Riehl (259). However, no time study was included nor information on man-hours. The author does conclude that the microfiche is more economical than microfilm when applied to documentation. Masters (373), in a paper describing experiences in microfilming archives at Exeter, included information on time required and costs in the copying of a miscellaneous collection of records. It was pointed out in the F.I.D. Manual (127, p. 221.3 E4) that microprint on paper will be cheaper than microfilm because 1. paper costs less than film and 2. in the case of microprint the fixed costs are usually spread over more copies. This same publication contains on p. 4E1-4E19 a fairly detailed treatise on the calculation of production costs of documents with useful charts. However, microcopying is not specially considered.

In a paper published in 1954, Fussler (131) stated (p. 38): "Since microfilming is a photographic process, its costs are commonly thought of as linear... This is not precisely true, but the original negative cost is always high... The negative may cost anywhere from 2 to 5 or 6 times the cost of a positive..." In a paper by Tyler and others (268), on the Kodak Minicard system, it was stated: "the cost of Minicards compares very favorably with conventional forms of punch cards and microfilm," but no further information on this point is given.

An accounting system for commercial microfilming firms was described by Fifield (374). Although not intended for non-profit institutions, if offers a detailed outline of cost factors in microfilming which could undoubtedly be adapted to cost accounting for library microfilm departments. Comparative costs of materials in 1956 for the several photoduplication processes were given by Ballou (148). Prices charged for microfiches, including negative and positive transparencies and opaque microfiches by Les Appareils Controleurs, Paris, are listed in Lewis and Offenhauser (143, p. 115). The prices are in French money and can be presumed to include profit. In other words, they are not production costs.

A variety of data on costs, most of it taken from published literature, was incorporated in a book by Lewis and Offenhauser (143). On p. 44-45 they reproduce a chart issued by Diebold, Inc. which pertains to the economics of storing versus microfilming of business records and estimates costs in dollars for equipment amortization, film cost, copy preparation, filming, and editing, including inspection, making corrections and packaging. This chart estimates two man-hours for copy preparation, one man-hour for filming, and two man-hours for editing and associated operations per file drawer.

On p. 47-51 they present an abstract and a table from U. S. Department of Defense, Army, Army Regulations 345-218, 23 August 1955, which provide information on costs of microfilming records in the Army and presumably in other governmental agencies employing Civil Service employees to do such work. The estimates of man-days are the same and are calculated on the same basis--that is, a four-drawer file cabinet of records--as in Reference 106, abstracted in part oh p. 26 of this report. However, the estimates of costs have been revised to conform with materials costs and salaries prevailing in 1954. The table provides a detailed breakdown of elements affecting costs of microfilming operations, with items grouped by operation and by relative cost. The latter grouping is not exact but consists of three classifications designated as "Least costly," "More costly," and "Most costly." The table applies primarily to record filming, but it could perhaps be adapted to an analysis of library microcopying. On p. 43 to 59 of their book, Lewis and Offenhauser give some information on costs other than that mentioned in the preceding two paragraphs, but it consists mainly of quotations of commercial prices for various microforms.

Pritsker and Sadler (375) in a M. S. thesis evaluating microfilm as a method of book storage in libraries gave costs per page and per linear foot of books for conversion of a library collection of books to microfilm. They used the storage library of the Columbia University School of Engineering in their study and found 4,600 pages per linear foot. This figure is the basis of their linear foot cost estimate. They warned against taking it as representative of all libraries or even for collections of bound journals. They show substantially different costs for copying with five different commercial cameras. The lowest cost was achieved with the RemRand Model 12, which uses 16 mm. film and has automatic feed. They found costs per page ranging from $.00111 to $.00476 as compared to estimates from commercial firms of from one to two cents per page. However, their costs do not cover profit, supervision or administration, office space, inspection or editing. They discussed editing at some length, pointing out that it is a slow, expensive process and giving six reasons (p. 292-293) why it is unnecessary in converting to microfilm a book collection such as the one studied.

Varden (149) presented comparative data on material costs for eight copying processes, including 35 mm. microfilm. In a discussion of very high reductions such as are necessary to produce microscopic documents, Stevens (151, p. 255-277) mentioned several factors that would make such operations costly but gave no data on the labor or money involved.

Preservation and Storage

Problems of maintaining and preserving motion picture film occurred in the motion picture industry some years before there was any significant amount of microcopying of documents. The technical journals on motion picture technology, therefore, contain numerous articles on the subject. Because most of this material pertains to nitrate film, no attempt will be made to include it in the present report. An article by Crabtree and Carlton (376) is an exception. It presents the results of tests made with various moistening and cleaning fluids on nitrate and acetate films, describes moistening and cleaning techniques, and presents formulas for fluids. It recommends for cleaning the use of sulphur-free and water-free carbon tetrachloride and describes a technique of removing water from commercial grades of this chemical.

Henry (18) discussed the problem of film storage from the librarian's point of view. He pointed out that in most cities ordinances required steel cases for the storage of film and that in some cities there were still prohibitions against storage of acetate film in any quantity in public buildings. Whether required or not, this author recommended steel cases and suggested "...a steel cabinet equipped with trays or drawers just deep enough to allow spools or reels to lie flat in them which means trays about two inches deep... These trays might be divided by partitions running from front to back." On p. 215 of the same article, the author described the use of concave shelves to hold long films in circular metal boxes, each box being about a foot in diameter and two inches thick.

In an article surveying the then new technique of copying newspapers on film, Brown (25) stated that projectors had been constructed so that there was no danger of blistering or burning of the film and so that the film was given maximum protection from wear. He was less optimistic on other factors of preservation. "Theoretically, film stored under proper conditions of refrigeration will last almost indefinitely; how far ideal conditions can be translated into library method remains to be seen."

Combining microfilm with cards or related types of support is a storage technique as well as one that facilitates retrieval. As early as 1934 Seidell (262) suggested the mounting of developed strips of microfilm in windows on cards and suggested suitable dimensions for the cards. In an editorial inspired by Brown's article noted in the preceding paragraph, Henry (26) gave more information on storage requirements of microfilm. He noted that no library should store cellulose nitrate film, and that its use in public buildings outside of metal booths or fireproof projecting rooms was prohibited by all municipal ordinances. In contrast, acetate film was permitted by most municipal codes without restriction. On the storage requirements of acetate film, Henry commented that such film deteriorates rapidly in a hot, dry room but is "believed to be imperishable" in a cool and humid place.

Henry recommended metal containers for storing the film and said that containers with a humidor pad on the cover were available from the Eastman Company. "A few drops of water placed on the pad every few minutes..." were supposed to maintain the essential relative humidity. Henry described a "cool, slightly damp vault" as ideal storage for films and stated that kept under such conditions they would suffer no deterioration. He recommended that at least once every five years they should be unwound, wiped with a cloth dampened with carbon tetrachloride and rewound.

In a report in which doubt on the permanence of microfilm was expressed, Kimberly and Scribner (29) stated (p. 25) that the ideal conditions of storage for safety film were a temperature of 50°F. and relative humidity approaching saturation. They stated that in a dry atmosphere cellulose acetate, or safety film, becomes brittle more readily than other types. Bendikson (31) discussed the restrictions (because of fire hazards) on the use of film projecting apparatus and the storage of film in libraries. He stated that to avoid infringement of regulations, film negatives should be shipped as soon as they are made, stored film should be kept in a properly constructed vault off library premises, and that films should be projected from a properly constructed projection room. He concluded that meeting the expense of fulfilling these requirements would be too expensive for most libraries and that the use of photostats would be more economical.

Seidell (39) referred to his earlier suggestion that film strips should be mounted in windows on filing cards and reported that it had proved too costly to equip projectors with holding devices for the cards. He accordingly made another suggestion: that the filmstrips be filed in envelopes. Determination by the U. S. National Bureau of Standards of the effects of environmental conditions on microfilm and specifications for its storage and use were among the needs mentioned in a symposium (38) devoted to the question of whether the time had arrived to preserve newspapers on film.

Bendikson (42) suggested two methods of storage for positive microprints on paper. For compactness, he recommended filing 5 x 8 inch prints in a filing drawer and stated that one filing drawer could easily contain 60,000 pages. The other scheme suggested was to print the negative film on paper strips of the same width as the film, then to fasten the paper strips to 15-inch wide sheets of thin Bristol, these sheets to be kept in small portfolios.

In a paper on the care of film in libraries, Weber and Hill (377) summarized the results so far obtained in tests still in progress at the National Bureau of Standards on the stability of cellulose nitrate and cellulose acetate films, then discussed at length the care of films and film slides and the effects of environmental conditions in libraries on them. They stated in this paper (p. 692) that acetate film presents no greater fire hazard than paper and that it had been found to be very stable if properly made and processed.

The effects of changes of moisture content on both types of film are described and relationships between relative humidity and flexibility are shown graphically. To avoid extreme brittleness of acetate film which occurs at a relative humidity of 15 per cent and below, they recommended (p. 694) "...some air conditioning precautions..." More specifically, they recommended a humidity of approximately 50 per cent. For libraries without air conditioning they suggested conditioning of a room with a small air conditioning unit or cabinets or small vaults for the storage of film. They gave specific directions for maintaining a relative humidity of about 52 per cent in a cabinet or vault by the use of a saturated solution of sodium dichromate exposed in shallow vessels with fans to promote air circulation.

They stated that acetate films should be stored in the conditioned chamber when not in use and stored as open reels without cans. Tightly wound rolls should be loosened and hung so that they would be exposed to the humidified air. They described several ways of restoring flexibility to acetate film that has become brittle. However, they said (p. 696) that film in card or strip form not subject to winding upon reels does not require moisture control if carefully handled.

The scratching of films in handling and in reading projectors was discussed. They implied that scratching could be reduced by better design of projectors and by keeping the films clean. However, they suggested that negative films of important records be carefully preserved to avoid damage by scratching. They recommended (p. 697) cleaning film with chemically pure carbon tetrachloride and regular inspection for dust, finger marks, and oil of films used intermittently.

According to a note in a column by Raney (378), the "Vaporate" process for preserving film was then being tested by the National Bureau of Standards and the Society of Motion Picture Engineers. This process involved placing the film while on the reel in a vacuum tank and withdrawing the moisture, after which two chemicals were introduced in the form of vapors to give the film elasticity and to produce a hard surface difficult to scratch. Metcalf (46) briefly described (p. 12) tests then being conducted on the permanence of film and the best storage conditions then being conducted by the National Bureau of Standards. He noted also that some investigators feared that acetate film will not last as long as nitrate, while others believed that it would. He said that considerable humidity and not too high temperatures were requirements for film storage and that special storage rooms should be available for maintaining these conditions.

Scribner (328), in a short review of National Bureau of Standards tests then in progress, stated that cellulose acetate films should be stored at a relative humidity of about 50 per cent. After being used they should be exposed to air of this humidity to restore lost moisture, and they should not be reused until moisture equilibrium had been retained. In an official report of the National Bureau of Standards (293) published in 1937, Kimberly and Scribner gave essentially the same information on humidity requirements and restoration of moisture, and added (p. 27) recommendations on the cleaning of film which were the same in substance as those noted in the second paragraph above from an earlier paper.

Metcalf (379) discussed storage and care at some length. His remarks on storage requirements appear to have been based on National Bureau of Standards publications. In discussing care he stressed the importance of protecting films from dust, recommending dust-free storage, clean projectors and occasional cleaning of the film with a velvet cloth dipped in carbon tetrachloride. He cautioned against overheating, tearing and scratching of the film. He discussed metal boxes, paper cartons, cartridges and cabinets with shallow drawers as storage containers and recommended containers that would make efficient use of library shelves.

In a paper based largely on New York Public Library experience, Fox (380) stated that special provisions for humidity control had not proved to be necessary in the climate of New York. Each reel of film was kept in durable paste board and ten of the individual boxes were stored in a larger paste board box of such dimensions that eight boxes fitted a standard 3 feet x 18 inch shelf. To guard the films against scratching the glass flats of the projector were carefully cleaned at least once a day. Films were cleaned by use of a "rewind" machine, arranged so that the film passed between pieces of heavy-piled, white plush which was saturated with chemically pure carbon tetrachloride. The film-feeding mechanism of the projector was covered at night to keep dust out of it.

Page and others (249) in a paper urging early standardization in microphotography recommended two forms: 1. reels for long lengths and 2. short strips containing up to ten pages of text. The strips were to be filed in envelopes which would be stored in the card catalog behind cards identifying the items on film. In another paper on standardization, Sayce (316) discussed the strip method of storage in more detail and described another method of storage which was being used at King's College. In this scheme up to ten strips were stored in a paper envelope 8-1/2" x 1-5/8" and the envelope, rather than a catalog card, bore the catalog entry, or other identifying inscription. The envelopes of film were stored on edge in drawers. In the same article Sayce discussed the inefficient use of space that is inherent in storage on reels.

The National Bureau of Standards' recommendations on relative humidity and temperature conditions for microfilm storage were reiterated in a survey (182) of microfilm equipment and supplies, then storage equipment was described. It was stated (p. 50) that containers should be designed for easy access and to protect the film against careless handling, to allow (p. 51) the film to rest on an edge rather than on the turns, and to allow the humidified atmosphere access to the film. Metal and cardboard containers for individual reels were described in general terms. Also described (p. 52) are miscellaneous storage devices such as a film wallet, transparent envelopes, a looseleaf folder and a number of commercially available cabinets. Experiments at the National Archives in laminating microfilm with thin sheets of cellulose acetate were mentioned.

Schüumeyer (74) recommended that films be stored in air-tight metal or plastic containers with screw tops and suggested that these containers could be kept on shelves or in drawers. Stauffer (180) described (p. 175) a system of storing film strips in transparent envelopes to avoid the scratching which occurs when film is used in rolls. Even with this added protection, he thought it advisable to make duplicates of the film strips. His paper was based on experience in the National Park Service.

In contrast to cutting roll film into strips for use and

storage, Carruthers and Wright (381) suggested splicing short strips together to form long, composite rolls. On the subject of care, these authors emphasized the importance of keeping clean those parts of the reader with which the film comes in contact and occasional cleaning of the film itself, the latter to be done by drawing the film through a compress of undertaker's plush which had been wet with carbon tetrachloride. They stated (p. 387) that their suggestions had been tested in use. Presumably the testing was done at the New York Public Library. Scribner (382) in a summary of research done at the National Bureau of Standards mentioned commercial preparations for making the emulsion on film harder and more scratch-resistant and stated (p. 20): "...a large number of treatments of this kind have been investigated...by use of a scratch-resistance test, but in no case has significant improvement been found."

Maurer and Bach (383) described simple, direct-reading gauge for measuring shrinkage and described the results of their studies of this characteristic of acetate-base films under various conditions of storage and use. They found that such film made by each of three U.S.A. manufacturers had a characteristic shrinkage which was ordinarily reached within a few days after processing and that subsequently shrinkage continued at a slower rate until an ultimate shrinkage of about 1.25 per cent is reached. This percentage was exceeded only in films exposed many times to high wattage lamps in projectors. Apparently, their studies were made on film manufactured for moving picture use. An announcement (384) was published of processes developed by American Recono, Inc. for the removal of scratches, abrasion marks, etc. from films. The purpose was to repair such damage after it had occurred, not to "scratch-proof" the film in advance.

In a paper read at an international conference, Metcalf (385) commented on the fact that many American libraries had not provided air conditioned storage or humidity control for microfilms, but had kept them under ordinary conditions, the recommendations of the National Bureau of Standards notwithstanding. In this connection, he referred to the belief that films made brittle by drying can be reconditioned. He described various containers then in use in U.S.A. libraries for the storage of microfilm. Brown and Austin (386) described a system of filing and storing film strips in standard 10" x 12" filing cabinet drawers. The film strips were placed in pockets on cards. The pockets, of which there were 18 to a card, were formed of tracing cloth or book binding cloth and details of forming them were given.

Film strips were kept temporarily in metal pillboxes 1-1/2" x 1-1/2" until enough had been accumulated to make a 75 to 100 ft. reel in a system described by Cibella (387). Eventually the strips were arranged in the alphabetical order of the names of authors of the copied items and spliced together to form a continuous reel. A system of labeling, filing and storing short lengths of 35 mm. microfilm based on the use of special devices sold commercially under the name "Filclips" was described and illustrated (388). The "Filclips" with the strips of film attached were stored in circular plastic or metal trays.

Specially made wooden spools 3/4" in diameter, a little over 7" in length, and with a flange at one end designed to serve as a base were used for the storing of short lengths of film in a system described by Jakes (389). Filmstrips containing from 3 to 50 frames were rolled to an inside diameter of 3/4" and five such rolls were placed one on top of the other on a spool. Twenty such spools holding five films each were stood in a friction top can measuring about 6" in diameter and 8" in height. Humidity could be maintained in the can by soaking one of the spools in water or by fastening a moist sponge to the inside of the lid.

Dice (390) described a method of filing filmstrips. Strips containing 4, 5, or 6 frames were filed in envelopes measuring 4-1/8" x 9-1/2". The envelope was divided inside into compartments by means of partitions and each strip had its own compartment. Identifying information was written on the outside of the envelope. In reply to a letter of inquiry, Fussler (391) described concisely the storage and care of acetate films. He stated that special storage is not essential and that the important things to guard against were dust and excessive ranges of relative humidity and temperature. He advised that if a special cabinet was provided and some control of humidity seemed desirable that a tray of water would be sufficient. However, he did mention that a saturated solution of sodium dichromate could be used to maintain a relative humidity of 50 per cent.

Power (392) furnished a description and illustration of a dust-proof, humidified cabinet in which pegs were provided for short lengths of film and drawers for 100-foot reels, and in which the relative humidity would be maintained at the proper level by sodium dichromate solution. Power suggested that the cabinet could be built by a carpenter. However, it was later manufactured and put on the market by a commercial firm. A detailed description of the commercial article was published (393).

Although not concerned with documentary film but with motion picture film used for archival purposes, the report (394) of the Committee for the Preservation of Motion Picture Film of the Society of Motion Picture Engineers contains useful information which is applicable to documentary film. Cleanliness is recommended in the handling of film, and specific recommendations are made, such as clean processing solutions, filtered air for drying, rounded corners and a minimum of furniture in rooms where film is processed and handled, wearing of lintless white gloves when handling film. It was stated that the most satisfactory liquids for cleaning films are carbon tetrachloride and light petroleum solvents, and that a mixture of petroleum solvent with carbon tetrachloride to reduce the flash point is often used. Humidity conditions which in conjunction with rapidly evaporating solvents cause moisture to condense on the film and produce glossy spots on the wound roll, are mentioned.

Crabtree and others (234) in a paper on hypo elimination pointed out that an increase in relative humidity, temperature or both will accelerate the rate of fading if residual hypo is present in the film and that a combination of high humidity and high temperature such as is found in tropical countries will destroy print containing hypo. They noted also that saline matter and acidic atmospheric gases tend to increase the rate of fading. Techniques of preserving and storing flat film microcopies were described by Reyniers (256). Contact prints of the original negatives were made; the positive prints were then treated by the Vaporate process to toughen the emulsion and render them scratch-proof. Titles were typed on adhesive-backed paper and stuck to the top of the microfilm. The negatives were stored in glassene envelopes.

In a paper devoted primarily to the "Color spool," Lilley (395) described and compared various schemes and devices for storing lengths of microfilm shorter than 50 feet. He viewed short strips 6, 9 or 12 inches in length, customarily filed in pockets on file folders or in envelopes or negative albums as unsatisfactory for library use. He pointed out that reading machines were not designed for short strips and that there was considerable risk of damage when strips were manipulated in them. In discussing the scheme of splicing short lengths together in order to form a long roll, he stressed the inconvenience to readers of searching for specific items and pointed out that the whole roll is exposed to damage when it is used for only a single title. Storage schemes evolved for short lengths of film cut into strips or spliced to form rolls are described. Separate aluminum or cardboard containers; larger containers to hold a number of separate rolls; large cans containing spindles; and storage cabinets with drawers and pegs are mentioned. Lilley noted as the chief objection to these devices that the films were not ready for immediate use, but had to be wound on an empty reel before reading, then unwound for storage.

In contrast, the Goler spool, which was simply a wooden core with detachable flanges was designed to hold the film both on the reading machine and when it was stored in cans or in cabinets. Since the film was kept on the spool at all times, it was ready for immediate use.

A description (396) was published of a microfilm storage cabinet introduced by the firm of Remington Rand. This cabinet was designed to hold film in storage boxes in nine of the drawers and a solution of potassium dichromate to stabilize humidity in the tenth drawer. The drawers were slotted to aid air circulation and the door was furnished with rubber gaskets to prevent escape of the humidified air. Storage procedures under varying conditions of humidity control including air-conditioned space, humidified cabinets, and the lack of any means of controlling the relative humidity were explicitly described in a War Department Technical manual (105). A leading manufacturer of microfilm for documentary purposes published a useful booklet (397) on the storage of microfilm and related microforms.

Bobb (340) described storage requirements partly derived from National Bureau of Standards publications and partly from established practice. He stated (p. 327) that negatives may be coated with 'Cinelac' manufactured by the American Bolex Company. This solution applied to the emulsion acts as a preserver protecting the negatives from scratches and finger marks. The British Standards Institution (398) published explicit recommendations for the storage of microfilm. Redepenning (107) in a general discussion of microfilm compared the storage characteristics of roll film and flat film. In his opinion roll film was more easily scratched and damaged in being rolled. Flat film, although subject to scratching, can be protected by placing paper between the sheets of film. Dust-proof filing cabinets were recommended for storage. A strip film system used at the Central Medical Library Bureau of the Royal Society of Medicine was described by Wilson (250). In this system, strips containing ten pages (frames?) are filed in numbered pockets of "po. chettes." The strips are filed in sequence so that, for example, no. 64 pocket contains the strip for p. 641-650 of the copied document.

Bacon (399) described the handling of microcards in the Library of Wesleyan University, of which Fremont Rider was then the librarian. They were filed separately from the public catalog in a classified arrangement. This differed from Rider's original suggestion that the microcard serve as the catalog card as well as the reading text. Modified Kardex type files were used to store 16 mm. microfilm strips in a system worked out in the Color Control Department of the Eastman Kodak Company. The system, described by Kuipers (286), was designed to meet the research needs of the Department and was based on the use of both microfilm and microcards. Stock-books--similar to those used by philatelists--designed to hold ten filmstrips, each 209 mm. in length, were described and illustrated in a paper by van der Wolk and Tonnon (119). Other storage devices in the same article are: plain envelopes and accordion-folded little books, both designed to hold microcopies in card or sheet format, that is to say, microcards or microfiches.

Microfilm storage and care were described in detail by Noll (400) in an article directed to librarians and archivists. He pointed out that microfilm is more delicate than paper. It is readily scratched, and the gelatin of the emulsion renders it very susceptible to damage by fungus growths. When brittle, it is easily broken. He cited the recommendations of the National Bureau of Standards on optimum conditions of relative humidity and temperature. He discussed at length the advantages and disadvantages of humidified cabinets and gave information on the difficulties which had developed in using these devices. He mentioned one manufacturer's film storage cabinet which had rubber gaskets on the doors and internal provision for good circulation of the air in the cabinet, implying that it was designed to avoid most of these troubles. He described explicitly procedures for maintaining a suitable level of relative humidity in cabinets where the control is chemical.

Noll advised periodical inspection of stored microfilm and described inspection procedures. Unusual odors, mildew, mold, rusty spools, discolored or faded images, buckled film, fluted edges and dust or fine powder were named as conditions to be looked for when examining the films. The author recommended consulting specialists whenever any of these conditions was found. He suggested not only inspection of the film, but also attention to such things as labels, order of rolls in the storage cabinet, replenishment of chemicals if humidified cabinets are used, and hazards such as hot radiators, steam and water pipes in the vicinity of the cabinets.

Storage requirements of microfilm were described in some detail by Würstlin (336), who recommended a relative humidity of 40 to 50 per cent and a room temperature of 18°C. to 21°C. Lower temperatures were noted as not being harmful, in fact, as better for color film, but relative humidity below 25 per cent should be guarded against. When films stored in cold places are brought into a warm room, precautions should be taken against condensation of moisture on them. Films must be protected from fire, water, damp locations, silverfish, gases such as hydrogen sulfide and carbon dioxide. Archival films should be stored in a space where the air is dust-free and the temperature and humidity are controlled. Acid-free cellophane pockets are suggested for the storage of film strips. Mention is made of protective coatings which have been developed for film, but none is explicitly described and the author advised awaiting the results of tests. Inspection of archival film at regular intervals and re-filming of any items even slightly damaged in storage are recommended.

It was reported (401) that the Postal Museum at The Hague possesses several of Dagron's microfilms made for the Pigeon Post. These films are preserved between glass plates which are sealed with Canadian balsam, obviously a method of storage suited to the preservation of films which are of extreme historic value. Offenhauser (217) in an article on the use of microfilm for the preservation of documents discussed storage and care among other things. He stated that storage should be planned to protect the gelatin of the emulsion and the film base from decay and suggested swabbing the film with fungus and bacteria-inhibiting compounds such as those sold under the trade names Merthiolate and Roccal. He stated that the emulsion can be hardened with formaldehyde which also inhibits the growth of organisms. He mentioned Vectograph lacquer made by the Polaroid Corporation as a suitable material for protecting the surface and sealing the edges of film.

Storage in a constant temperature away from exposure to light were noted as desirable, but the author pointed out the maintenance of temperature within a narrow range is costly both for equipment and operation. Even with good storage he expressed doubt about preservation of specific pieces of microfilm longer than 50 years and suggested for record preservation a three-stage procedure under which original films would be kept in dead storage under the best conditions, intermediate copies would be kept in live storage under the best possible conditions but would be used to make copies. Copies made from intermediates were to be used and when not in use were to be stored under the best "day-to-day conditions." He recommended an engineering approach to microfilm preservation designed to provide the best storage and care that can be afforded for original copies while making other copies available for use.

Shaw (319), in a paper devoted to the potentialities of machines in documentation, supplied comparative data on the storage capacity of various machines and devices, "books, punch cards, Elliott stencils, Addressograph slugs, reduced facsimiles, catalog cards, notched cards, Univac, 35 mm. film at usual reduction ratios, microcards, 16 mm. film at same reduction ratio as microcards, Rapid Selector." The comparisons were based on a standard 250-page book measuring 5-1/2" x 8-1/2" and containing 100,000 words. It is shown in terms of cubic inches the span required for storing this book in the various forms and devices mentioned.

Microfilm was surveyed for archivists in a memorandum from the Public Record Office of Great Britain (402). Standard information on durability, washing to remove residual hypo, testing for residual hypo, temperature and humidity requirements, etc. was given. Regular inspection at intervals of at least once a year was recommended so that any deterioration from residual chemicals or fungus attack could be detected at an early stage. Ventilated boxes were recommended for the storage of reels if temperature and humidity were controlled. Lacking these controls, it was suggested that films be conditioned by exposure to an atmosphere of the correct humidity for 12 hours, then placed in an air-tight container. Envelopes, special folders with pockets and card index cabinets were suggested for the storage of film strips, microfiches and microcards. Storage of unit boxes and envelopes in larger boxes of dimensions that permit convenient storage on standard shelves was suggested, but the availability of special storage cabinets was mentioned.

In a comparison of the cost of storage of documents in conventional form and in the form of microfilm made by the Organization and Methods Division of the British Treasury (372), it was stated (p. 35) that none of the studies made by the Division showed an advantage in storage space requirements that approached the figure of 90 per cent reduction found in unnamed books and leaflets. Instead, it was found that 35 mm. microfilms when packed and stored occupied approximately 1/26 of the space required for the original documents. It is shown in the paper how this figure was obtained. In the same paper, it is pointed out that when films are used for archival purposes expense is incurred in making the films available to the public and examining them before returning to storage.

A vault designed to be proof against bombs but also providing optimum conditions for the storage of microfilm which was built by a large industrial corporation for the safeguarding of microfilm copies of its engineering drawings was described by Darling (403). Power (260) described a storage system developed for preservation of microcopies of clipping files of the New York Times. The clippings had been copied on 70 mm. film which after developing, had been cut into pieces. The pieces were inserted into acetate envelopes and identifying information was written on the envelopes with a special-formula acetate ink. Envelopes were designed so that the film could be placed in the reading machine and read without removing it from them.

Ballou and Rather (247) discussed at length the storage of microfilm in both the ribbon and sheet formats, pointed out that the first is related to movie film and the second to the photographic print. In contrast, mechanically printed micropaper is merely paper and ink. The storage "climate" best for all is composed of a temperature range of 60°F.-80°F., a relative humidity of 40 to 50 per cent and an atmosphere free from dust and acidic gases. The authors pointed out that this is a good climate for people, too. They recommended periodic inspection and cleaning of the film, periodic cleaning of reading machines, "diplomatic observation" of readers while using the films, and judicious restriction on the accessibility of sheet film and micropaper.

They suggest reels containing 100 feet or 50 feet if the film is used often, and reels of 1,000 feet or greater capacity for master films used seldom. They state that pill boxes for short strips have decreased in popularity because of administrative problems and suggest instead pocket files originally developed for miniature camera enthusiasts. Envelopes or sleeves of paper are recommended for sheet microfilm. Warnings are given about paper containing chemicals that will have a deleterious effect upon film and envelopes with seams that will catch. They stated that films should be inserted with the emulsion side away from the seam to protect the emulsion from the adhesive. They pointed out that side-seamed envelopes caused "fanning" of the file, while center-seamed ones put the seam next to the data-bearing portion of the microsheet. The envelopes with the films may be stored in cabinets similar to card cabinets.

These authors pointed out that microcards having photographic emulsion on one side only tend to develop a concave curl. This tendency can be counter-acted by storage under pressure, but pressure may lead to abrasion when cards are withdrawn and inserted. Neither Microlex cards nor microprint sheets tend to curl and both are furnished with storage cases.

In a pamphlet on the handling of special types of material in libraries, Collison (404) briefly described (p. 33) containers, boxes for film strips (presumably rolled), and gave dimensions for a six-drawer cabinet. On p. 17 he discussed metal, "usually aluminim," containers for the storage of microfilm and referred to British Standard 1153, 1944 for details of standard construction. He pointed out in passing that this Standard recommends the storage of microfilm on one of its edges, but most libraries continue to store it vertically. He described and gave the dimensions of a five-drawer cabinet with built-in provision for the chemical control of relative humidity. In a book published in the same year which was a revised and enlarged edition of a book published in 1950, Collison gave essentially the same information on storage of film strips and roll film, but included pictures of different cabinets.

Jacobson (405) reported the results of a ten-month study on the maintenance of humidity in a Yawman and Erbe microfilm file cabinet. Except for a few days at the beginning of the test, a saturated solution of sodium dichromate in the cabinet maintained the relative humidity at 50 per cent, with no apparent effects on the finish of the cabinet. He quoted from a letter from the National Bureau of Standards on the desirability of reasonably air-tight, humidified cabinets, then discussed the management of cabinets in which the humidity was controlled by sodium dichromate solution. He pointed out that in a dry atmosphere, including heated rooms, the water will evaporate and require replenishing, but in the summertime during periods of high humidity, the solution will take up water and some may have to be removed. An excess of undissolved sodium dichromate must be present at all times for the solution will not act as a dehumidifying agent unless saturated. In fact, under some conditions an unsaturated solution may even give up moisture in sufficient quantity to cause the film to become damp and promote the growth of fungus.

Léauté (224a) in a discussion of preservation and storage of microfilm contained in an article on standardization of the base devoted considerable space to varnishes for protection against scratches, repair of scratches, and protection against attack by microorganisms. He stated that such varnishes had been developed for the protection of color films, and certain of them were suitable for microfilm. A formula for such a film is included in the paper. He showed that keeping of film at less than 50 per cent of relative humidity disturbs the transverse curve formed in the course of manufacturing and whose purpose it is to make the image side of the film slightly concave. He emphasized also the danger of attack by microorganisms when the relative humidity exceeds 55 per cent and recommended the use of protective varnishes containing fungicides.

In an article based largely on experience and experiments of the United States Air Force Motion Picture Film Depository, Baumhofer (406) described ideal storage and the effects of conditions not ideal, such as too high temperature and humidity. He stated that temperature variations in the lower ranges are not so dangerous as too high or too low humidity, and mentioned experiments in which films were kept in an outside shed at the University of Alaska for two years without bad effects, while films stored in a chamber where the temperature and humidity were high showed chemical deterioration, shrinkage, rusted cans, fungus infestation, etc. after three months. Nitrate film is kept in "breather" cans to permit gas fumes to escape, but safety film is kept in tight-fitting round or square cans. Stainless steel or plastic reels were recommended for permanent storage of roll film.

The author noted that storage in a vertical position was recommended by fire authorities so that in case of fire, water will run down the sides of the can and drain away. However, the author noted that if films are stored long in this position, they sag and the layers on the inside adhere to one another and therefore they are usually stored flat.

The book by Lewis and Offenhauser (143) contains various information on preservation and storage. On p. 38-39 it is suggested that frequently used microrecords should be cut into frames or short strips and enclosed in protective cards or jackets. On p. 185 they recommend that some form of protective coating be applied to protect the film from scratches and that when the coating becomes damaged to the point where it interferes with a high quality image, it should be removed and a new application made. They mention also a harder type of coating solution obtainable through the Peerless Film Processing Corporation which has been widely used, but state that it is impractical to remove this type. They state further that hardening agents, such as are commonly used in the fixing bath, are often sufficient protection for end-use films. On p. 327-333 they reproduce the proposed American Standard Practice for the Storage of Microfilm, first draft dated December 2, 1954.

Experience with the storage of microfilms on regular libary shelving at Harvard College Library was the basis of a paper by Weber (407), who described mainly a method of film storage in boxes. Boxes of metal-edged fiberboard were especially constructed for the purpose by the Hollinger Company of Arlington, Virginia. Each box was designed to hold six standard microfilm reels. Inside dimensions were 10" x 4" x 4" and the author notes they should have been 1/4" longer and perhaps 1/8" larger in the other dimensions. Their use made it possible to store 864 reels on regular library shelving in "a regular 40-inch book section." Costs are given and comparisons are made with other storage systems for film. A proposed standard for the storage of microfilm originating with Committee PH5 of the American Standards Association was published (408).

Care in handling photographic negatives and prints in libraries was discussed by Luecke (409). Although photographs on a scale that does not require the use of readers or projectors rather than microcopies are dealt with, the methods described are in large part applicable to microfilm, especially sheet microfilm, as well. It is recommended that each negative be kept in a separate envelope or jacket which has been manufactured for the purpose. A warning is given against ordinary envelopes which may stain the negatives. Also it is pointed out that the seam of a special negative jacket is located at the side to prevent the gum seal from touching the image on the film, and that the jacket is manufactured so that no glue is on the inside and so that the interior is dust-free. Negatives should be handled by the extreme edge and clean white cotton gloves should be worn handling them, especially in a hot climate. Common sense directions about keeping water, ink, coffee, paper clips, etc. off negatives are included.

The area required in terms of square feet for two makes of commercially available microfilm storage cabinets, the Remington Rand and the Yawman Erbe, was stated and compared (p. 293) of a paper by Pritsker and Sadler (375). A system developed for the microreproduction of large-scale engineering and architectural drawings included an interesting storage device (254). The negatives were made on 105 mm. roll film, which after developing was cut into 4" x 6" frames. Each of the frames was placed in a transparent sleeve, then frame and sleeve were placed in a paper envelope for filing. Presumably the negative was to be read or projected without removing it from the transparent sleeve.

Retrieval and Enlargement

In the beginnings of documentary microcopying, retrieval seemed to present no special problems. The films or film slides were to be projected on screens for reading or enlarged prints were to be made from them. As to keeping the films in order and identifying them, these matters would be simple too. In his first article on the subject published in 1932, Henry (18) suggested (p. 217) that reels might be labeled on their ends, drawers containing them might be marked with a generic designation such as "Greek Manuscripts" and within the drawers the spools might be arranged according to the classification system used by the library.

In an article published the next year, Henry (23) reported that Harvard University was prepared to make 5" x 7" and 8" x 10" enlargements from its negative microfilms of manuscripts. The William L. Clements Library was making "full size prints" from its films and was experimenting with a machine for making postal-card size prints which could be read with a reading glass. On p. 239 of this article, Henry discussed projecting and mentioned several projectors, including enlargers, adapted for making enlarged prints and for projecting the image on a screen for direct reading.

Two methods of retrieval were mentioned by Björkbom (154): 1. the negatives were printed on paper and the microprints read with a binocular microcope, and 2. they were enlarged to 105 x 148 mm. or 210 x 295 mm. for reading without optical aid. The author pointed out that the microphotographs could also be projected with a lantern. Projection was the method of retrieval proposed by Goldschmidt and Otlet (8) in their historic paper published in 1907. Projection apparatus is described and illustrated in the discussion of microcopies in Otlet's treatise on documentation (28). Projection by means of existing projecting machines (presumably lanterns) was the method of retrieval envisioned by Seidell (262) for his proposed aperature cards containing film strips mounted in windows cut in cards.

Bendikson (31) pointed out that film projecting apparatus could not always be used in libraries because of conflict with fire prevention authorities and regulations. Although it could be used in private dwelling, a film projector was a "cumbersome method of reading, collating texts or consulting books..." His preferred solutions to the problem of retrieval were 1. low reduction microprints on paper which could be read with a magnifying glass or binocular microscope, and 2. economy photostats which were photostat copies produced at a reduction ratio which reduced standard-size book pages to about three inches in height, but left them legible without optical aid.

Otlet (27) described an invention by Georges Sébille which is fully described in French patents 673,365 and 696,287, and U.S. patent 1,889,575. Sébille's scheme included placing macroscopic numbers or letters in the margin of the film and a means of rendering them legible while the film was being wound at full speed. Otlet mentioned also that Sébille was working on a machine for automatic calling up of desired frames or passages.

In an article published in 1935, Seidell (39) referred to his earlier suggestion (262) of aperture cards for film strips and said that the high cost of equipping projectors with holding devices for the cards had made the idea impractical. He suggested instead that the film strips be filed in envelopes with the necessary bibliographical information on the outside. In the same article he suggested photographing on the first frame of a strip the journal title, volume page, and year in a style sufficiently large to permit reading without optical aid. Johnson (37) in an article describing copying experiences in European libraries with a 35 mm. camera discussed the problem of making the microreproductions readable. He stated that the negatives could be projected, or a positive could be made by contact printing and the positive projected. He indicated that some scholars preferred enlarged prints and gave the opinion that satisfactory enlargements of printed material could readily be made from Leica negatives. He suggested further that if frames were grouped for enlarging, the expense of enlargement would be greatly reduced.

Van Iterson (53) experimented with low ratios of reduction. His microcopies could be read in part with the unaided eye and in entirety with a hand reading glass magnifying 203 diameters. The prints were stored in 13.5 x 22.5 cm. envelopes. Saint Rat (61) proposed keeping film strips in slots on cards measuring 215 x 14 mm. The film was to be held in place by being covered with transparent cellulose acetate. Three strips, each 200 mm. long corresponding to 30 pages of text, were to be stored on each card with the bibliographical listing of the copied article on the verso of the card. In the same article he proposed as an alternative plan keeping the strips in a box shaped like a book.

Vanderbilt (410), in a report on experiments carried out to find a solution to certain problems in connection with the development of a union library catalog for the Philadelphia metropolitan area, described a small enlarger specially built to make 6.2 x 10.3 cm. enlargements on 7.5 x 12.5 cm. cards from microfilm. The author was unable to give exact specifications for the enlarger, but stated the lens was a small "f 1.9" and the degree of enlargement was 12 diameters. He mentioned also enlargements at 8 diameters made by the Eastman Kodak Company which were one-half the size of the original cards but were quite legible.

Sébille (411) discussed his efforts toward development of an automatic catalog in which the information, catalog entries or microcopies of documents, were stored on strips of 35 mm. film 5 to 20 meters long. He gave some figures on the capacity of the film, for example, a strip 15 meters long would hold 20,000 images, each image being a reproduction of four catalog cards. The principal features of the device (see also Reference 23) were a combination of macroscopic, numerical or alphabetic indexing on the film margin and a system of moving mirrors to project the indexing symbols on a screen as the film is wound or unwound at full speed. He proposed an automatic system for calling up the frame or page desired, but did not describe the technical details.

Hodgson (69, p. 246) stressed the importance of having on microfilms and other forms of microcopy identifying information in a size readable without optical aid. He mentioned particularly title page, table of contents, classification or location marks, ownership marks and an indication of the scale of reduction, as desirable information to have in a readable size. Carruthers and Wright (381) described methods tested at the New York Public Library for classifying and numbering microfilms. The primary identification mark was made up of a film symbol followed by a serial number. Also included were such ideas as a notation on the carton showing the sequence of items on the enclosed film, if the film contains more than one document, and a label on the end of a case to show the numbers of the handling "open entry" films, that is, incomplete film copies of serials, to which additions will be made. They pointed out the convenience of having at the beginning of each film strip or reel a photograph of a placard giving in a macroscopic scale, the author, title, date, place of publication, location of the original and the reduction ratio used for the film copy.

It was pointed out in a survey of microfilming published in 1938 (182) that two kinds of indexing of microfilms are necessary, identification and page locating. The first gives the source of the material and "some portion of a scale or rule." An abbreviated notation on every frame of film is recommended (p. 48). Schemes for page or item locating are surveyed and described, including the Teledex type of locating by means of large index letters and a rotating prism which causes the index letters to appear almost stationary on the reading screen, a system sometimes called stroboscopic indexing. Other systems described include one evolved by Merle C. Gould which utilized photo-electric cells and a keying system and another system which employed flash indicators inserted between every hundred frames.

It is emphasized (p. 49) that

> ...every effort should be made to prepare a micro-

> film which should be as usable as the original itself and a number of suggestions toward this goal are made, such as filming the index and table of contents of a book at the beginning and end of the film and including on the film a portion of a rule or other scale to indicate the original size of the book or document copied.

A research study of indexing and page location in microfilm was recommended.

Johnson (175) in an account of a long experience in copying documents as an individual scholar mentioned both reading glasses and enlargements as methods of retrieval. Usually he made 6" x 10" or 8" x 10" enlarged prints and assembled them to make bound volumes. Brown and Austin (386) described a simple method which combined a catalog on standard cards with numbered file cards and numbered pockets on the cards.

Various features of sheet microfilm pertinent to retrieval were mentioned by Bennett (255), particularly "a natural convenient sectionalization of the material; a system of filing which makes every unit immediately accessible; a means of identification which is integral with each unit and can be read without optical aid." A decimal arrangement of the images on the sheet, that is to say, ten rows of ten pages per row reading from left to right, was mentioned by Tennant (297, p. 69) as a feature of Readex Microprint. In a paper on public record microfilming, Noll (412) described a system of indexing which included numbering the pages of records to be copied with automatic numbering stamps; an index sheet which was photographed at the beginning and/or end of the reel, and a reduced negative photostat of which was mounted on the outside of the carton; and diagonal stripes on the cartons to indicate misplaced cartons in storage drawers. Another interesting suggestion was the use of perforations on the film to indicate omissions and emendations.

As an aid in the identification of films, Bobb (340) suggested numbers to indicate various combinations of page exposures and placement on the film; also, macroscopic images "Start" and "End" at the beginning and end of each document copied; following the word "Start" the introduction of a title card showing the name and address of the institution making the film and the date of the filming; a copy of the order form or other sheet giving the title of the material filmed and any restrictions on its use. He suggested also photographing a centimeter scale in juxtaposition to the document and rephotographing it at every change in size of the original.

Moholy (97) made reference (p. 63) to British Standard 1153-1944 as making provision for large rolls, small rolls and strips and proposed still another method of storing microfilm: the filing of strips containing microcopies of articles and passages under subject headings, an arrangement which she termed a combined "Index-and-File." Indexing schemes for microfilm in the United States War Department were described in Technical manual 12-257 (105). These included space targets photographed on the film at intervals of 100 cards, alphabetically arranged indexes of names, cross reference sheets, punched cards, labeling procedures for cartons, etc. These schemes as described are particularly suited to the retrieval of microfilmed records, but some of the ideas are applicable to collections of documentary microfilm.

Perforations in the film corresponding to page numbers and positioned so as to operate a counter on the reading machine were suggested by Redepenning (107). This author noted that flat film has an advantage in this respect because one sheet will hold images of 60-100 pages, the numbers of which can be noted at the top of the sheet. Wilson (250) mentioned a camera which photographs the title and pagination of the copied document on the margin of the film as an aid in retrieval.

Several indexing and retrieval schemes were described by Bobb (207) in an account of the uses of microfilm in a war agency. For some uses individual microfilm frames were inserted in square apertures on punch cards, while the balance of the card was used for indexing purposes by punching it. Needed films were then selected by running cards through an IBM automatic selector. An index was made to rolls of film and was used in full size and also microcopied at the end of the roll. A rod sorting scheme was used to index separate 2-1/4" and 3-1/4" negatives cut from 70 mm. microfilm. Cards for the index were made by making a contact print of each negative upon 4" x 5" card stock or on double-weight photographic paper. The border of the card was then punched with holes and selected holes were then opened to the margin of the card to indicate specific data contained in the microcopy. Selection was made in the usual way for such sorting schemes, that is to say, rods were passed through the pack in a pattern corresponding to the code for the needed data and cards, punched to correspond, then fell free when the file was manipulated.

A working party of the Royal Society's Scientific Information Conference (244) included (p. 272) in a report on the merits and proper fields of application of various microforms a long comment on the inconvenience of using long rolls of microfilm. They discussed the difficulty of finding needed frames, especially in looking up cross references, and the time wasted in changing from one reel to another. Also, they pointed out (mistakenly) that continuous film does not allow the interpolation of new items and, therefore, cannot be kept in classified or alphabetical order.

Forsdyke (211), commenting on this paper in the same volume (p. 702-704), pointed out that rolls of film were not as long as implied. He said that the maximum length used for documentary microcopying is ordinarily 100 feet, and that most books and manuscripts are copied on a film less than 35 feet in length. He stated further that irritation that develops in searching for specific frames on roll film is not due to the time involved, but to the fact that the user cannot see what he is doing while moving the film. To correct this he suggested the photographing of a large pilot number at every fiftieth page, and the copying of the index of the book immediately after its table of contents. He said that frames can be interpolated by splicing at any point on continuous film, but that this should not be done on films initially divided into standard lengths, nor should it be attempted on a scale appropriate to a card index.

In a system for filing microfilm strips in envelopes developed by the Science and Technology Project of the Library of Congress, the following information was put on the face of the envelope to aid in retrieval: "...full cataloging information, an abstract of the document, appropriate subject headings, and a number which is also reproduced on a microfilm strip" (252). Jolley (114) described a system of retrieval in use in a college library which included a microfilm accession register. For each film an accession number was entered in the register and was photographed at the beginning and end of the film. In addition, the accession register served as a record of the date of making the film, the source of the copied material, the contents of the film, and notes on its quality and conditions of photography. To find the location of an item on a reel which contains a number of documents, it is necessary to consult the microfilms accession register. The author discussed numbering of the items and numbering of the frames, but said that doing so would slow up the photographing too much.

The Rapid Selector was the outcome of undoubtedly the most significant effort to solve the problem of the rapid retrieval of information from microfilm. Its history is outlined, and the principles and objectives of electronics selection were authoritatively discussed by Shaw (413) who was one of the key figures in the development of the Rapid Selector. Shaw credited Dr. E. Goldberg with the first practical application of electronics to the selection of data on film and Dr. Vannevar Bush with the basic principles of organization of knowledge and the basic electronic system used in the Rapid Selector. He showed that the Rapid Selector takes advantage of well known electronic principles, but applies them to the selection of data. He outlined three broad areas in which electronic selection and reproduction of data might be useful: the reduction of space required for the storage of information; cumulative indexing of various sources as in a literature search through numerous periodicals and improvement in the organization of knowledge for administrative routines and communication among scientists. The last mentioned area is described as the most important and a considerable part of the paper is devoted to exploring the potentialities in it of electronic selection and particularly the Rapid Selector. Technical details are mentioned only incidently.

The technical details and numerous illustrations of the Rapid Selector were made available in a report (414) by the designers of the components of the first machine. This report also contains an outline of the devélopment and states that the Rapid Selector is similar in basic concept to the Bush Rapid Selector which was announced by the Massachusetts Institute of Technology in 1940. Description of technical details was combined with operation and maintenance instructions in a report issued by the Office of Technical Services of the Department of Commerce (415). A cluster of articles on the Rapid Selector appeared in various journals in 1948 and 1949. Only a few will be mentioned here.

Green (416) pointed out that the primary difference between this Rapid Selector and the earlier one was the system which signalled the machine to make reproductions of selected frames. In the new machine the significant areas in the coded pattern in the margin of the film were black. To cause the machine to select and reproduce the appropriate frames, a coded black mask with holes corresponding to the desired code pattern was inserted in a photoelectric monitor device. When a coded pattern on the film corresponding to the code on the mask passes before the mask, light to the monitor was cut off and this constituted the signal to the camera to make a reproduction of the frame marked with the selected code. This novel system was described in many of the articles which appeared on the Rapid Selector. A descriptive article (417) addressed to librarians was supplemented by some notes by Shaw. An illustrated, semi-technical account was published in a journal addressed primarily to engineers specializing primarily in electronics (418).

The librarian of a large civil engineering firm described (419) the indexing and retrieval system used by her firm when it copied drawings on microfilm to save storage space. When the original drawings were prepared for microfilming, 2 x 2 feet sheets of drawing paper bearing such notations as "1 to 50," "51 to 100," etc. and also the inclusive catalog numbers were inserted between each lot of 50 drawings. The designations were of a size that made them stand out clearly as the film was run through the projector. A separate card catalog provided the information that the drawing had been microfilmed, the number of the roll containing the microcopy and the numerical location of the drawing on the roll.

Microcards, since they bear full catalog entries on one side and may be filed and interpolated in the manner of standard card catalogs, do not present the problems in retrieval associated with microfilm. Rider's original proposal (274) was that the microcard would be the catalog card, but it was soon found that this was impractical in the average library primarily because in order to read the text the microcard had to be removed from the catalog for reading and its removal took away evidence that the library possessed the microcarded item. In a paper by Bacon (420) describing the handling of microcards in the library of Wesleyan University, it was shown that microcards were then filed in a separate room from the public catalog, they were arranged by the Library of Congress classification, and within classes by author entry. The author suggested that in libraries using the Decimal Classification, the cards would be filed by D. C. number.

In a broad survey of flat film in documentary microcopying, van der Wolk and Tonnon (119) rendered the opinion that

J. A. Reynier's method of putting the title of the copied document on the film by photograph was superior to P. G. Violet's method of putting it on a separate card which was joined to the microcopy by a strip of adhesive tape.

Shaw (421) described a new camera theoretically capable of taking up to 500 pictures per second intermittently. It was designed for use with the Rapid Selector and its purpose was to eliminate much of the expensive optical and electronic mechanisms which had been necessary in order to slow down the film when closely spaced frames were selected for copying. The camera mechanism is described in detail and is illustrated. Shaw's paper concludes:

> The new camera represents a step forward in converting the Rapid Selector from an experimental machine to a practical and economical tool for day to day use. A considerable amount still remains to be done before a cheap and practical selector can become generally available, but the principles are proven and the improvements and simplifications required appear to be in sight.

Engstrom (422), writing for chemical engineers, discussed the problem of rapid selection in information work and described the Rapid Selector, which he viewed as a step in the development of "a device of true flexibility." Shaw (423), in a paper discussing machines and bibliography, summarized again the development of the Rapid Selector and the contributions made by various persons. Discussing the advantages of the machine, he stated (p. 60) that it "...uses approximately two hundredths of a one per cent of the space required for comparable storage and indexing of the originals. Furthermore, the selector provides for instantaneous reproduction of copies..." The paper contains further illuminating discussion of the Rapid Selector (and by extension other machines of the kind) for information retrieval. Another important point made (p. 45) is that while schemes for great reductions in space occupied by documents, for example, the placing of many books on a single card, have received much attention, the primary problem in documentation in our age is retrieval of information.

In another paper, Shaw (318) analyzed bibliography making and retrieval of information from a management viewpoint. He showed (p. 208-210) that the great speed of machine selecting often mentioned is a fallacy when applied to searching of large collections of information and stated (p. 210):

> If machines are to be used for bibliographic purposes, then more attention will have to be paid to the other elements of getting an answer from a selected block of information that requires much more attention to the question of getting the logically selected block of information into the machine and getting the answers out of the machine, and less emphasis on the running speed of part of the machine...

The Rapid Selector is described as to its fundamental principles and method of coding, its advantages in information retrieval are discussed, and the author states (p. 223):

> In general it would appear that the Rapid Selector opens up the possibility of coupling the advantages of microfilm for storage with simple and speedy electronic sorter, so as to make possible economic use of microfilm for storage, finding and reproduction of bibliographic entries or text...

Vickery (424) took issue with Shaw on two basic points: the degree of saving in storage space made possible by the Rapid Selector, and the speed of location and reproduction. He presented a diagram or flow sheet of the process of locating information and used it for reference in his discussion. Using the selected run of chemical abstracts and the comparison indexes as an example, he reached the conclusion that the saving offered by microfilm is not as spectacular as suggested by Shaw, but is worth considering. Again using Chemical abstracts as an example, he found that the difference between searching a long series of abstracts with the Rapid Selector and searching them manually in the usual way was not as great as had been stated. His final conclusion on this point was:

> It is only for searches which throw up hundreds of references that the Selector offers any outstanding advantage in speed; ...the locating of references which high-speed selection facilitates is only one step in the process of "information retrieval," and takes up only a small percentage of the research time involved.

A device much more limited in capacity than the Rapid Selector was described by Schulman (425). It was developed by the Western Union Telegraph Company for company uses.

In it strips of microfilm were formed into closed belts and mounted on chains and sprockets. An index to the microfilm was mounted on a drum which was connected to the chains in such a way that turning the drum also rotated the belt of film. The light source and lens system was placed in such a way that the microcopy on the belt was projected onto a screen for reading or reference. Potential applications to library purposes were not discussed.

Concise but detailed accounts of the Rapid Selector and Samain's electronic punched card selector were included in a general discussion of possible mechanization of bibliographical control by Jamieson (426), who discussed also such devices as high-speed electronic computers which do not necessarily employ microfilm. Of Samain's device it is stated (p. 218):

> Samain uses what he describes as an 'artificial vocabulary...of abbreviations and miscellaneous conventions'... Having analyzed a document and decided its coding, the code is then punched into a card from a keyboard similar to that of a typewriter... A photoelectric scanning device replaces the needle and brush devices of commercial machines as the method of interpreting the perforations on each card... Essentially then, the Samain selector is a high-speed locating device for items of information, depending for its accuracy upon an electronic scanning unit, in principle not unlike that of the Bush-Shaw machine...

Reference is also made to Samain's French patent 928,340, Nov. 25, 1949.

In a comparison of the leading types of microcopy, Boni (299) stressed the decimal arrangement of pages on the microprint sheet; that is to say, ten rows of ten pages each, always in the same sequence, as an important feature which makes possible the rapid location of references. One scheme of combining microcopy and punched cards as an aid in information retrieval was described by Williams and Rose (265). The scheme involved using ten columns of the standard card for decimal or other classification number and ten for a code of randomly spaced four-digit random numbers representing the data on the card. Cards were to be coded and sorted in standard IBM machines.

Schürmeyer (427) described "Selecto," a coding system

developed by G. Cordonnier, a system not limited to the indexing of microfilm but suitable for such use. Cards representing references to papers, books or to microfilms are filed in numerical order year by year, and each one is assigned an arbitrary number within the year. A second file of subject cards is coded in the margin. The system appears to be a modification of "peek-a-boo" sorting. Combinations of punch cards and punch card coding with microfilm to facilitate information retrieval were described by Knigge (428) who presented information on a number of European and American punch card systems.

Filmorex, an electronic selection system for microfilm, was described in a booklet (429) issued by its inventor, and in an article (430). The components of this system are a two-lens camera which simultaneously copies a document in one-half of the width of a 72 mm. film and a code of transparent and opaque dots in the other half, 72 x 45 mm. microfilm units which are made by cutting up the film after developing, and an electronic selector which scans the coded half of the units at the rate of 600 a minute. Selected units are automatically ejected. After sorting by the machine, the selected units may be read in a reader, printed off in actual size, or reproduced by standard methods. The units or microsheets are economical of storage space and are not readily damaged. It is claimed that millions may be selectively sorted by the machine in a brief period of time.

Enlarging practices were briefly described in Bastardie's summary (214) of Verry's survey, where it is stated that there were not many models of microfilm enlargers on the market. It is pointed out in the same discussion that many microfilm readers may be used to make enlargements. Production of enlargements with automatic equipment in Great Britain and the United States was mentioned, and it was stated that since this method requires a large volume of work, its use is not general.

Several significant articles on mechanical and electronic retrieval were published in 1953. Gull (431) discussed the growing use of instrumentation in libraries of the national government under the pressures of an increased volume of source materials and demands for wider and more extensive services. He included microcopying, discussing making of microcopies, uses, and selecting devices for use with microcopies, including the Rapid Selector and commercially developed system such as Keysort, Rocket, Pathfinder and E-Z

Sort. U.S. Patent 2,594,358 was issued on the Rapid Selector, the full text of which was published by the U.S. Patent Office. An abstract appeared in the Library journal (432) as well as in other journals.

The Automatic Micro-Film Information System was described in Special libraries (433) and an abstract of a mimeo graphed report on it issued by the inventor appeared in American documentation (434). A capacity of 1-1/2 million documents or 9 million catalog cards was claimed for this system, the basic mechanical components of which are described in U.S. Patent 2,610,791. It is arranged so that by operation of the keyboard a frame can be selected and the image projected onto a viewing screen, or the frame can be reproduced by photographic techniques or Xerography. The system was said to possess exceptional selecting speed in addition to permitting browsing as with a standard microfilm leader.

Verry (435) discussed electronic and mechanical retrieval devices in general but with particular reference to the Rapid Selector and Filmorex developed by Samain. He described also the Film "N" Sort system which combines microfilm and punched card sorting. The paper was written primarily for information of readers who would be interested in such devices from the administrative viewpoint. The author concludes "...that high speed electronic selection will play an indispensable part in the growing need for greater speed and ease in the selection of scientific and technical data."

In a paper describing the history, activities, equipment and methods of the Photoduplication Service of the Library of Congress, Holmes (133) mentioned automatic enlarging from microfilm, saying that microfilm enlargements were being made by Kodagraph continuous enlargers at the rate of 40 feet per minute, and that the exposed paper is automatically processed.

Niven (436) described a new apparatus developed by the Photostat Corporation for making enlargements from microfilm. Shaw (437) in a short paper briefly described the principles of operation of the Rapid Selector, pointed out the same three areas of potential application as he had described in a paper (413) published in 1949 and stated that the application of machines for bibliographical purposes depends upon the development of adequate statements of bibliographical requirements and systems for utilization of machines and management of the literature.

Shaw (438) analyzed the steps in preparation of bibliographies from the viewpoint of possible mechanization. He dealt only by implication with microforms, but did say (p. 526) of the Rapid Selector (which, of course, searches microfilm):

> While copying is always a purely mechanical operation, of all the machines proposed or available only the selective addressing machines and the Rapid Selector provide for copying the citation directly and automatically as part of the searching process... Of all the devices now known, the Rapid Selector is the only one that provides for automatic copying of the data as part of the search process.

The Kodak Minicard System (268) includes mechanical and electronic sorting and selecting and the handling speed was estimated at 1,800 cards per minute. However, it appears that the sorting and scanning machines were not yet developed. In a demonstration held in June, 1955 at Rochester, a machine for simple sorting was shown and a prototype scanner was used to illustrate some operations that the scanner will perform when development is completed.

Titling, an essential step in preparation for retrieval of microcopied information in practically all of the simple systems is discussed by Lewis and Offenhauser (143, p. 173-174). Procedures are described, useful information is included on heights of letters, making of title cards or placards, and photographing. Two illustrations show a title prepared with movable letters on a "menu board" and a title prepared with an IBM electric typewriter. Chapter 9, "Information Classification and Retrieval," of Lewis and Offenhauser's book presents a reasonably detailed survey of the subject with literature references. The Rapid Selector is concisely described on p. 288 and the authors stated: "The potential for such a device is the recording of vast amounts of information that requires compact storage which must be available on demand." The Filmorex system and the Automatic Microfilm Information System are described in the same book on p. 288-289. On p. 289-290 there is a mention of a photoelectric scanner developed at the Massachusetts Institute of Technology in collaboration with the International Business Machines Company which operated on punched card scanning up to 1,000 per minute in literature searches.

Retrieval aspects of Readex microprint are discussed on p. 105 and p. 301-303 of Lewis and Offenhauser's book, where the decimal arrangement is described and it is also pointed out that microprint may be classified or arranged chronologically. Microcards are discussed from the same viewpoint on p. 303-304. Various methods and techniques of labeling and indexing microfilm are described on p. 306-318. These include stripes, colors, and labels on reel cartons, guides, targets and indexes photographed on the films, various systems of putting titles on microfiches and other forms of sheet microfilm, the labeling and indexing features of Filmsort cards and combinations of microfilm with margin-punched cards. Illustrations are included of many of the devices.

Enlarging from microfilm is covered on p. 198-225 of the Lewis and Offenhauser treatise. They described both equipment and procedures. However, the descriptions are concise and more suitable for general information on the topics covered than as guides to actual practice. Methods of making enlarged copies with readers are described and simple equipment produced by the Recordak Company for this purpose called "Rapid Facsimile Kit" is mentioned. Also included are descriptions of some direct copying devices which may also be used for the rapid production of readable though not high-quality enlargements from microfilm. Among the last mentioned is Kalfax, a dry process which is capable of enlarging 14 to 20 times in about 30 seconds from microfilm.

Retrieval features of a microfile of geologic material were described by Reed (269). The finished microcopies are sheet film in the shape of 5" x 8" cards with a hole code punched on one edge for needle sorting. Cards are grouped in eight major groups. Each group has a distinctive groove-location in the top edges of the card so that if a card is misfiled, it breaks the continuity of the groove.

A data storage and retrieval device developed in the Electronic Instrumentation Laboratory of the National Bureau of Standards was described (439). This device, termed Automatic Microimage File, employs 10" x 10" sheets of microfilm. Ten thousand frames containing reproductions of documentary material or of coded data are photographed on each sheet. The machine automatically searches the sheet and prints out selected frames containing sought information.

Summary and Suggestions for Further Study

The established state of microcopying, primarily as it appears from the preceding literature survey, is concisely summarized in this part. Also presented here are outlines of proposed research projects in areas where study and investigation appear to be needed. The summaries of the art appear first, and are followed by the outlines of needed research.

History of microcopying. When this report was written there was no published comprehensive history of microcopying, although areas of the field, for example, Dagron's work and the Pigeon Post, had been covered in a satisfactory scholarly fashion. However, announcement had been made of a forthcoming comprehensive history of microcopying by Frank Luther. In view of the excellence of this scholar's already published historical studies, probably no further major work on the history of microcopying will need to be done for some time. Furthermore, the literature survey presented in Part I should serve as a guide to most of the important ideas and devices which have been proposed and developed.

Equipment and materials. For several reasons the section of this report which deals with equipment and materials for microcopying is not complete. Although there are exceptions, manufacturers' literature has, in general, been ignored. The patent literature and the technical literature on photography have not been systematically searched. The literature on readers and projectors has been omitted according to plan.

Professional library literature was searched for information on equipment and materials and some information was taken from the technical literature of photography. Although the result is reasonably comprehensive because most important developments (and some not so important) in equipment and materials for microcopying are eventually noted in the professional library literature, this survey is not complete enough to serve as a sound base for recommending needed research on materials and equipment. One cannot say, for example, that there is need for research directed toward the development of a film emulsion with specified characteristics, for such an emulsion may already have been described in a patent though not placed on the market.

However, there appears to be no large gap in equipment or materials for the making of microcopies on film as microcopying is currently done in the average library photographic laboratory. Microcopying cameras have reached a state of development which permits most operators to produce clear images at the reduction ratios currently employed and the available film materials are very reliable. More automatic features in cameras are always desirable up to the point where the material to be copied could merely be handed to the camera, which would search out the needed pages, automatically select the exposure time, automatically take the necessary pictures, then close the book and hand it back. However, practical improvements in cameras are often made. The potentialities of automation in enlargers are great; and, in fact, elaborate, automatic equipment for such operations as the enlargement of microcopies of engineering drawings have been manufactured, but these are too complex and costly for most library needs. An office machine (on which no literature reference was found) recently introduced by the Minnesota Mining and Manufacturing Company is more suited to average libraries. This machine permits viewing as in a reader the successive images on a microfilm, then the prompt semi-automatic making of an enlargement when a desired frame is found.

Some of the larger laboratories, such as that of the Library of Congress, have from time to time designed special equipment, or have been instrumental in having it designed commercially. In such cases the need for the equipment has often arisen from a specialized operation performed by the laboratory, such as the rapid reproduction of catalog cards. Most new techniques and some improvements in techniques create needs for new equipment and materials. For example, if sheet film in microfiche form or some other convenient shape should supersede roll film for short runs of microcopy, there would be a need for an inexpensive, portable camera that could be used by individual scholars in copying on sheet film. However, effective suggestions for research directed toward the development of equipment and materials can only be made after the need is clearly apparent.

Some needs cannot be fulfilled because a basic invention is still needed. A typical demand of this kind is for dry methods of microcopying and enlarging from microcopies. However, there is already much effort on the part of commercial firms as well as by individual inventors to develop dry copying methods for use in governmental and business applications. Such methods for microcopying will undoubtedly come (when they do) as a further development of successful dry methods for office copying in identical or slightly reduced sizes. Because of such aspects as these, no research project directed toward the development of equipment or materials for making microcopies or for making enlargements from them is suggested in this report.

Photographic methods. To a large extent the photographic methods employed in microcopying are refinements or extensions of methods developed in conventional photography. The special requirements of microcopying led to the development of specialized cameras and was a major factor in the development of fine grain film. Vibration-free cameras with optical systems capable of filling microframes with clear images and fine grain film which permits the degrees of enlargement now accepted in microcopying have long since been available. The special films now available for microcopying are satisfactory and reliable products. The large manufacturers of photographic materials and equipment, such as the Eastman Kodak Company, constantly do research that bears on microcopying and will probably be the source of major developments.

There is much discussion in the literature of reduction ratios of the order of 1:200, 1:300, etc; and microcopies at such extreme reductions have been made and enlarged back to legible copies. Reduction ratios of this order are not commonly used, but enough is known about their requirements to justify the assumption that extreme reductions could be made practicable if there was a need for them. In this partially developed area there seems to be need for research to determine the advantages that would accrue from high reduction ratios for various types of use and thus to determine the level of effort that would be justified in developing this field.

Types and characteristics. To draw a somewhat clumsy analogy, microcopying is in a similar state of development to automobiles prior to World War I. The general outline of the art is clear, but there are still many divergent lines of development. Furthermore, no one type or form is sufficiently dominant to prevent new forms being introduced and enjoying some commercial success, though success may be temporary. As a further complication in this area, the main lines of development have been different in Europe and in the U.S.A. In Europe sheet microfilm is favored and has reached a fairly high state of development, but in the U.S.A. film in ribbons and rolls has predominated.

Another major divergence is between paper and film as bases for the microcopy. In fact, there are so many diverse forms, both established and proposed, that a concise summary of them is not possible. Verry's survey conducted for Unesco and the present survey based on the literature describe the many types and forms. A research project designed to clear up some of the confusion in this area of microcopying is outlined later in this section.

Quality factors. Quality of microimages has been discussed in the literature at least as much as any other aspect. Early in the modern development of microcopying librarians were concerned primarily with durability of the film base and the stability of the image. Extensive research by the National Bureau of Standards has resulted in tests and criteria for durability and stability and the role of residual "hypo" in image deterioration has been thoroughly studied by others. Reliable tests for residual hypo and standards for minimum tolerances have been promulgated and widely accepted. Problems of durability and stability of standard microfilm have thus been reduced to problems of maintaining vigilance on the part of processors and users. Procedures for testing and statistical quality control of microfilm have been explicitly stated by Lewis and Offenhauser, as noted on p. 122-123 of this report.

Reduction ratios in relation to quality have been the subject of numerous studies and papers. Nevertheless, this area of the field is full of apparent contradictions. Numerous authors have indicated that reductions of about 1:16 are the highest which are consistent with quality. On the other hand, Kodak Minicards employ a reduction of 1:60, and it is stated (see p. 93 of the report) that legible prints can be made from sixth generation copies. Study is needed to determine the reduction ratios most suitable for various uses. Very high reduction ratios of the order 1:300 have been mentioned from time to time in the literature, often with the implication that they offer great advantages in documentary microcopying. This idea has been discussed critically by

Stevens (as pointed out on p. 94 of this report), who concluded that such high reductions could not be made commercially, at least by present-day methods, and that they were justified only when the need was great to keep the bulk and weight of the microcopy at a minimum.

The development and publishing of standards has become a specialty in the world of technology, pursued by specialist organizations operating nationally and internationally. In the field of microcopying, much work directed toward the development of standards has been done outside the official organizations. However, at present the International Standards Organization and the leading national organizations, such as the American Standards Association and the British Standards Institution, have committees or subcommittees who are concerned with standardization of microforms.

Published standards often include glossaries of related terms. As more standards are published, these glossaries tend to become the official terminology of the field. Well-sponsored, unofficial glossaries, such as the one compiled by the National Microfilm Association's Committee on Terminology (135-136), usually contain the terms which have appeared in standards, together with other terms in use though not yet accepted as standard.

Because of the activities of the standardizing associations and the National Microfilm Association, as well as such agencies as the American Library Association's Committee on Photoduplication and Multiple Copying Methods in Standardization and Terminology, additional research does not appear to be needed in these areas at the present time. However, a research project on the overall problem of quality is proposed later in this section.

Production costs. It has already been pointed out (see p. 105) that there is little information in the literature on the costs of producing documentary microcopies. Information on charges made by libraries both at the present time and in the past is readily obtainable, but there is sound reason for doubting whether these charges are rationally related to production costs. Some of the studies which have been published on production costs were made in the days of $1.00-per-hour wages, and are much out of date on both labor and materials costs. Other studies, for example Pritsker and Sadler (375), omit important cost factors such as supervision and editing. Published studies contain useful ideas on factors to be investigated, but none was discovered which could be directly applied to typical microcopying operations in the U.S.A. at the present time. A research project on production cost factors is discussed later in this section.

Preservation and storage. Storage requirements for microfilm were studied early in the modern development of microcopying by the National Bureau of Standards. The results of these studies have been made available in several publications of the National Bureau of Standards (293, 328, 331, 334, 337). The British Standards Institution published in 1944 and 1955 (398) Standard recommendations for microfilm storage. Still another publication in which storage requirements are summarized in a useful manner was issued by the Eastman Kodak Company (397) in 1946. Environmental requirements for storage of microforms on cellulose acetate bases are now well understood, despite the fact that not all library microfilm is stored under the recommended conditions. There is much less information on the storage requirements of microforms on paper bases.

The literature is replete with schemes and devices for holding microfilm in storage. Most of these have developed out of the experience of individual librarians or libraries. Many devices have found their way to the commercial market. Those which have found buyers in sufficient number are still available. One can buy containers of various sizes and styles for roll film, envelopes for strips and composite forms, cabinets for the storage of reels, etc. In comparison to other types of equipment such as cameras, storage devices are easy to design and bring to the status of commercial availability. Homemade devices seldom present undue difficulties. Despite this ease of development research on storage devices seems to be needed to determine optimum devices.

The idea of applying a solution or varnish to film in order to prolong its life is one that dies hard. Treatments of this kind were devised almost as soon as the early nitrate motion picture film began to deteriorate. Since then there has probably been no period when several such treatments were not being promoted commercially. Nevertheless, no solution or coating has yet gained recognition as being useful in the preservation of documentary microforms. In 1939 the National Bureau of Standards reported that it had investigated a large number of treatments of this kind, but had found none that significantly improved resistance of the film to scratching. No later reports of the National Bureau of Standards on such treatments was found. This needs further study.

Retrieval and enlargement. The making of enlargements from microfilm of good quality is a procedure in photographic technique. There are a few problems peculiar to microfilm such as compensating for micro-images of different quality on the same strip or reel, but the solutions to these problems also are photographic. Enlargements may be made in very simple ways, for example, by exposing photographic paper in a microfilm reader, or they may be made with elaborate automatic machinery. The machines now in use are undoubtedly subject to improvement. At one end of the scale readers might be better designed for making enlargements; at the other end there might be in the commercial enlargers more built-in automatic compensation for variations in the density of the microimages. However, improvements such as are needed will undoubtedly be made as designers and manufacturers of photographic equipment see an adequate market for new or improved machines. No research project directed toward the development of enlargers is suggested.

In contrast, retrieval, aside from mere enlargement, is a vast field in which much inventing and development has already been done without production of practical devices that fully meet the need. Even among the simplest of retrieval devices, those which indicate or index the contents of reels, there is no uniformity. Every situation brings forth its homemade scheme, usually without reference to other schemes already developed to meet similar needs. Matters, such as whether when a complete book or pamphlet is microfilmed, the table of contents and index should be copied on the film preceding the text, can eventually be settled by the publication of standards under the auspices of such organizations as the American Standards Association.

Slightly more complex problems, such as a method of reading page numbers while a microfilm is being spun rapidly through a reading machine, will be solved by the emergence of a scheme or device which is so superior to others that it will gain wide acceptance. Several promising inventions have been directed toward solving this problem. In addition, there are simple unpatented schemes, such as the photographing of a number in macroscale at stated intervals on the film. A research project designed to sift the various schemes and devices which have been proposed or tried might produce useful results.

Very rapid automatic or semi-automatic selection of desired references or information from reels of microfilm or from other microforms containing a multitude of entries is an objective shaped by the informational needs of present-day society. Devices such as the Rapid Selector, Filmorex, the Automatic Micro-image File, and the Kodak Minicard System are all attempts at filling a need which is felt in every technical library. Since none of the devices of this kind yet invented has filled the need, a research project on automatic retrieval is outlined later in this report.

Proposed Research Projects

Project A. There is a great multiplicity of microforms. Many varieties have been devised for specialized uses in business and government. However, even in the area of documentation and library economy, there are numerous competing forms: roll microfilm and strip microfilm (both in several widths), sheet microfilm (in numerous sizes and image arrangements), microcards, Readex microprint, and reduced facsimile. Forms such as Microlex, though not prominent in the library picture, are capable of library use. The present survey and Verry's survey of microphotography for Unesco (120, 212) will provide sufficient evidence of the abundance of forms together with descriptions of them. The hindering effect of the multiplicity of forms on international cooperation and use of microcopying in documentation has been discussed in numerous papers.

A parallel effect on the use of microcopying within nations has attracted less attention, at least in the published literature. Nevertheless, it is a fact that large libraries are now required to purchase several types of readers in order to use the microforms that they purchase, and few libraries purchase all types. Few, if any, library photocopying laboratories are equipped to make all of the microforms currently used. Individual scholars who make use of microcopies in their homes or laboratories are handicapped by the multiplicity of forms and the lack of a reading device which will accommodate all or even several types.

It is proposed that a research project be organized to examine critically the various microforms, both those which have been proposed and those which have gained some measure of acceptance. The object would be to find answers to such questions as: What microforms are necessary? What is the extent of use of each type--nationally, internationally? Would dropping of some types result in increased use of others? If approximately three types were selected for survival, could their dimensions and forms be correlated sufficiently so that a single kind of reader could handle all of them?

This project should consider such aspects as convenience, cost, durability, and relations to retrieval problems. Without doubt, it should make a thorough investigation of the comparative merits of sheet film, such as the microfiches, and ribbon film, such as standard microfilm. The reasons for the European preference for the former should be carefully investigated, for undoubtedly in the U.S.A. the balance is tipped toward the ribbon forms by the large manufacturers of photographic materials.

Project B. It is an obvious fact that quality in microcopies costs money, as in any manufactured product. Another fact equally obvious is that desirable qualities in microcopies made for the preservation of valuable records are different from those required in microcopies made for ephemeral use by individual scholars. If a microcopy is to be used within a month after it is made, then thrown away, there is little point in taking precautions to remove residual hypo. In the area of legibility, materials such as engineering drawings containing important numerals require more care in microcopying and enlarging than straightforward text written in the common language.

Although there has been a fair amount of writing on such matters and some of the published national standards set up standards for residual hypo, legibility, etc., there is no comprehensive, uniformly accepted scorecard for quality factors in the various kinds of microcopies and for various uses of them. Availability of such a scorecard would benefit both producers of microforms and users. Firms such as Readex Microprint could use it as a guide to prevent the production of copy too illegible for its intended use. Users who need microcopies of permanent record quality would benefit by a systematic statement of desirable quality factors; while, on the other hand, scholars who use microcopies as a substitute for hand copying and throw the copies away shortly would benefit by not having to pay for the quality factors essential in record microcopies.

It is proposed that a project be set up to tabulate and

rate or evaluate the quality factors for each type of microform now in use and further to indicate which factors are important in the various categories of uses of each microform. The object would be to produce, in the form of a poster or booklet, a guide or a scorecard that could be followed by both producers of microcopies and users.

Project C. Although costs have been a problem ever since libraries began to make microcopies for individual scholars, few cost data have been published which are currently useful. There are several reasons for this state of affairs. Early in the use of microcopying by libraries, the microcopies were looked upon as substitutes for interlibrary loans. Costs were not considered in making interlibrary loans--why figure them in making microcopies? Seidell in a paper (89) published in 1941 debated whether scholars should be charged at all for microfilm copying since they were not charged for library services rendered when using libraries in person.

The multiplicity and diversity of factors in microcopying costs (see for example, p. 110 of this report), and their variations from one institution to another have made difficult the analysis of costs on anything resembling a general basis. In many instances, cost studies which have been published have been rendered in terms of material and labor costs prevalent at the time the study was made rather than in the more useful terms of materials used (and wasted) and man-hours. Despite the considerable range of information which has been published on costs (see p. 105-121 of this report), a thorough study of cost factors is still needed and is here proposed.

The study should be concerned with cost factors in the day-to-day production of microfilm copies in typical microcopying laboratories. It should produce a thorough analytical breakdown of all cost factors in what could appropriately be called routine library microcopying. It should not be concerned with costs on large projects such as the microcopying of a large card catalog, nor with unusual projects such as the filming of old and fragile files of archives. It should have as its major object the eventual reduction of charges for microcopies made for individual users.

Problems which appear to require special study are the cost of bringing books to the microfilm laboratory in the typical large library; whether readers who themselves bring the books to the order desk or laboratory should be charged less; whether the typical $1.00 minimum charge per volume is justified in the light of costs; and whether overhead and bookkeeping costs which are admittedly a large share of the costs of filling small orders can be reduced. On the last-mentioned point, something might be learned from the methods of mail order houses, such as the Doubleday Dollar Book Club, which apparently make a profit on small orders in spite of bookkeeping costs. Possibly the coupon system used by the United States Patent Office offers a solution to the bookkeeping problem.

Another question worth investigating is whether cost factors would permit lower charges to customers on orders not requiring prompt service. In other words, if the customer indicates that the filling of an order can be deferred for several weeks or months if necessary, will cost factors permit a lower charge? This could well be the case if deferred orders could be held until several accumulate for one publication or one serial set.

Whatever the direction or extent of the study, its findings should be stated, insofar as possible, in units that will not go out of date; that is to say, in units such as quantities of material used, quantities wasted, man-hours, fringe benefits as a percentage of man-hours, shipping and mailing costs as a percentage of man-hours on typical orders, etc.

Project D. As early as 1936, Metcalf (46) pointed out that the making of short runs of microcopy for individual orders would always be expensive because of overhead clerical costs, and he proposed as a solution a central organization which would maintain a master file of negatives from which prints could be made on order, thus avoiding the costs of bringing original documents to the laboratory to fill individual orders and making it possible to use the best automatic machinery in making prints and enlargements.

Metcalf's proposal has the appearance of being one of those important ideas which is introduced before the time is ripe for it. When it was published, the pressures for rapid and extensive documentation which exist today were not pronounced. In fact, they were comparatively nonexistent. Furthermore, wages and fringe benefits which now contribute so much to the cost of filling orders for microfilm were much lower. The demand for microcopies was also very much less. In short, there was not the need for centralization of microcopying in 1936 that there is today. It is proposed that the idea of a centralized organization to build up a file of master microcopies, to fill orders for copies from the masters and to serve as a center for retrieval, be thoroughly investigated.

The multitude of library microcopying laboratories owe their existence primarily to the origins of library microcopying. As already pointed out, microcopying was viewed as a way around lending documents on interlibrary loan. As the use of microfilm grew, it remained a logical arrangement for each major library to maintain a laboratory for the copying on order of its own materials. Nevertheless, it is the very essence of microcopying, particularly microfilming, that copies can be made at a distance from the original material once a master copy has been made.

The attractiveness of the idea of a central organization derives both from the superior service that could be rendered and from the fact that efficiency and economies are often much more easily achieved in a large organization than in a small one. This research project could be advantageously related to Project C on costs and to Project E on retrieval.

Project E. The demands of our times for information, especially in the fields of science and technology, have pointed up the inadequacy of what might be called hand methods of documentation. Speedy mechanical or electronic retrieval appears to be the only possible solution to the problem. The needs in this area have not been overlooked by inventors and other thinkers. Devices such as the Rapid Selector (413, 414, p. 145 of this report), the Automatic Microimage File (439, p. 153 of this report), Filmorex (429, 430, p. 150 of this report), the Automatic Micro-Film Information System (433, p. 151 of this report), and the Kodak Minicard System (268, p. 152 of this report), have been invented, fully described, and in several cases carried to an advanced stage of development. However, they have not come into wide use. Perhaps what is needed is an entirely new invention. A critical examination of the existing inventions and ideas, combined with a detailed statement of desirable features, might break the log jam and bring one or more of the devices into practical use.

The job should be done as soon as possible, because the type of microform used in the retrieval machine should be similar to or identical with the type used by individual scholars in order to facilitate the use of microcopy. In short, what is envisioned is a research project that would 1. critically explore the needs for rapid large-scale retrieval from microfilm or other form of microcopy, 2. critically examine the leading inventions and devices already made or proposed, and 3. point out the gaps that need to be filled or the needed inventions.

References

History of microcopying.

1. The Athenaeum, no. 1341, p. 831, July 9, 1853.
2. Brewster, David. The microscope. Encyclopedia britannica, ed. 8, 14:801, 1857.
3. Luther, Frank. René Dagron and the siege of Paris. American documentation, 1:196-206, 1950.
4. Dagron. [Prudent R.-P.]. Traité de photographie microscopie. Paris, 1864.
5. Willemin, M. Micro-photography. British journal of photography, 12:152, 1865.
6. Lefevre, Julien. La photographie et ses applications aux sciences, aux arts, et à l'industrie. Paris, 1888.
7. Fabre, C. Traité encyclopédique de photographie, v. 4. Paris, 1890.
8. Goldschmidt, Robert and Paul Otlet. Sur une forme nouvelle du livre; le livre microphotographique. Institut international de bibliographie, Bulletin, 12 année, p. 61-69, 1907.
9. Goldschmidt, Robert and Paul Otlet. Le livre microphotique. Institut international de bibliographie, Publ., no. 144, p. 1-8, 1925.
10. Rossignon, René. Appareil "Noxa" pour la photographie d'objets et la reproduction, l'agrandissement ou la reduction de tous documents. La société d'encouragement pour l'industrie nationale, Bulletin, 124:790-794, 1925.
11. Seidell, A. The Berthelot centenary and the resulting international efforts to advance chemistry. Science, 67:497-499, 1928.
12. International committee on intellectual cooperation. Minutes of the tenth session July, 1928. League of Nations, Publication, Series 12 A7, p. 47, 120, 122, 1928.
13. International committee on intellectual cooperation. Minutes of the eleventh session July, 1929. League of Nations, Publication, Series 12 A3, p. 106, 1929.
14. Clerc, L. P. La photocopie. British journal of photo-

graphy, 76:681-682, 1929.
15. Reko, Victor A. Reproduktionen aus büchern. Minerva zeitschrift, 6:113-116, 1930.
16. Binkley, Robert C. Methods of reproducing research materials. Chicago, 1931.
17. Half million documents filmed for Library of Congress record. United States daily, 6:709-710, 1931.
18. Henry, Edward A. Books on film: their use and care. Library journal, 57:216, 1932.
19. Eder, Josef M. Geschichte der photographie, aufl. 4, Halle, 1932. p. 544-547. (Eder, Josef M., History of photography, translated by Edward Epstein, New York, 1945. A translation of the fourth German edition.)
20. Bendikson, L. When filing cards take the place of books. Library journal, 58:911-913, 1933.
21. Case, C. Z. Film files would outlast newsprint. Editor and publisher, sect. 2, p. 111, 1933.
22. Wines, W. E. Preservation of newspapers by photography. American newspaper publishers association, Bulletin, p. 697-699, 1933.
23. Henry, Edward A. Films versus books. Library journal, 58:238-239, 1933.
24. Binkley, Robert C. Place of reduced scale copying in library policy. American library association, Public documents committee, Public documents, p. 219-222, 1934.
25. Brown, Karl. Newspapers on films. Library journal, 59:471, 1934.
26. Henry, E. A. Newspapers on films. Library journal, 59:468, 1934.
27. Otlet, Paul. Le livre photomicrographique. I.I.D., Communicationes, 1 [2]:19-20, 1934.
28. Otlet, Paul. Traité de documentation. Brussells, 1934.
29. Kimberly, A. E. and B. W. Scribner. Summary report of the Bureau of Standards research on preservation of records, U. S. national bureau of standards, Misc. publ. 144, Washington, D. C., 1934.
30. Scribner, B. W. Preservation of newspaper records. U. S. national bureau of standards, Misc. publ. 145, Washington, D. C., 1934. (Also published in Paper trade journal, 99:167-171, 1934.)
31. Bendikson, L. The place of photography in the reproduction and preservation of source material. Library journal, 59:548-549, 1934.
32. Van Asperen, J.P.C. Neuzeitliche photographische reproduktionesverfahren. I.I.D., Communicationes,

1 [3]:1-12, 1934.
---- Erganzungen und verbesserungen. I.I.D., Communicationes, 2 [1]:16-19, 1935.
33. Binkley, R. C. New tools for men of letters. Yale review, 24:519-537, 1935.
34. Case, C. Z. The status of experimentation with the film-slide method of reproducing documents. American library association, Committee on public documents, Public documents, p. 223-229, 1935.
35. Duyvis, F. Donker. La photocopie micrographique sur papier. Office international de chimie, L'Utilisation du film comme support de la documentation, Paris, p. 21-27, 1935. Also published in I.I.D., Communicationes, 2 [2]:16-22; and with additions as Publ. 127 of the Nederlandsch institute voor documentatie en registratuur.
36. Gillot, R. Quelques problemes posés par la reproduction de documents sur film cinematographique. Office international de chimie, L'Utilisation du film comme support de la documentation, Paris, p. 21-27, 1935.
37. Johnson, Rozelle Parker. The use of a 35-millimeter camera in European libraries. Library journal, 60: 293-295, 1935.
38. Kuhlman, A. F. Are we ready to preserve newspapers on films? A symposium. Library quarterly, 5:189-214, 1935.
39. Seidell, A. Film-strip copies of scientific publications. Science, 81:174-176, 1935. Reprinted with additions in U. S. department of agriculture library, Agricultural library notes, 10:69-73, 1935, and in I.I.D., Communicationes, 2 [2]:24-27, 1935.
40. Tate, Vernon. Micro-copying as an aid to research and the preservation of source materials. American library association, Public documents committee, Public documents, 1935, Chicago, 1936, p. 210-217.
41. Barnett, Claribel R. The bibliofilm service. U. S. department of agriculture library, Agricultural library notes, 11:55-60, 1936.
42. Bendikson, L. Microphotography in the Henry E. Huntington library and art gallery. American library association, Microphotography for libraries, Chicago, 1936, p. 88-92.
43. Carruthers, Ralph H. Seventy millimeter paper and its place in photographic reproduction. Library journal, 61:912-915, 1936.
44. Davis, Watson. Microphotographic duplication in the

service of science. Science, 83:402-404, 1936. Also published in American library association, Microphotography for libraries, 1936, Chicago, 1936, p. 47-52.

45. Binkley, Robert C. Manual on methods of reproducing research materials; a survey made for the Joint committee on materials for research of the social science research council and the American council of learned societies, Ann Arbor, 1936.
46. Metcalf, Keyes D. Micro-copying on photographic film. Library journal, 61:10-15, 1936.
47. Patterson, E. F. Application of small scale photography to library purposes. Library association record, 38:347-51, 1936.
48. Pratt, Verneur. The micro-copy film situation. Library journal, 61:260-263, 1936.
49. Raney, M. Llewellyn. Microphotography notes. American library association, Bulletin, 30:893-895, 1936.
50. Schellenberg, T. R. Microfilm copying of documents. Society of motion picture engineers, Journal, 27:90-93, 1936.
51. Simplification program films. Library journal, 61:681, 1936.
52. U. S. Library of Congress, Report of the librarian of congress for the fiscal year ending June 30, 1936, Washington, D. C., 1936, p. 40.
53. Van Iterson, J. G. On the preparation and reading of printed matter. I.I.D., Communicationes, 3 [IT]:1-4, 1936. Substantially the same article appeared in several other journals.
54. Saint Rat, L. de. Le microfilm appliqué à la documentation scientifique. Société d'encouragement pour l'industrie nationale, Bulletin, 135:669-676, 1936.
55. Duyvis, F. Donker. The International federation for documentation. Journal of documentary reproduction, 3:176-191, 1940.
56. Fussler, Herman H. Library photography. Library journal, 65:115, 1940.
57. Tate, Vernon D. Microphotography. The complete photographer, 7:2530-2566, New York, 1942-43.
58. Pollard, A. F. C. Miniature and microscopic documents. British society of international bibliography, 5:43-54, 1943.
59. Stevens, G. W. W. Microphotography since 1839. Photographic journal, 90B:149-156, 1950.
60. Luther, Frederic. The earliest experiments in microphotography. Isis, 41:277-281, 1950.

61. Saint Rat, L. de. Micro-documentation filmée. Revue scientifique, 74:752-758, 1936.
62. Grant, John. Books and documents. London, 1937, p. 189-192.
63. Rush, Charles E. The foreign situation in microphotography. American library association, Microphotography for libraries, 1937, Chicago, 1937, p. 1-12.
64. American library association, Microphotography for libraries, 1936, 1937, Chicago, 1936, 1937.
65. Tate, Vernon D. American progress during the year. American library association, Microphotography for libraries, 1937, Chicago, 1937, p. 13-38.
66. Fussler, Herman H. Progress in microphotography in the United States. Congrès mondial de la documentation universelle, 1937, La documentation...., Paris, 1937, p. 124-128.
67. Schürmeyer, W. Die fotokopie im dienste der dokumentarischen arbeit. Congrès mondial de la documentation universelle, 1937, La documentation..., Paris, 1937, p. 299-304.
68. Raney, M. Llewellyn. First steps in microphotography, 1938. American library association, Bulletin, 32: 164-166, 1938.
69. Hodgson, James G. Microcopying essentials (from a librarian's point of view). Journal of documentary reproduction, 1:243-262, 1938.
70. Page, B. S. and L. A. Sayce. Introduction to microphotography. Library association record, 40:16-18, 1938.
71. Binkley, Robert C. Techniques and policies of documentary reproduction. I.F.D., 14th Conference, Transactions, p. C121-C124, 1938.
72. Tate, Vernon D. Peculiarities of microphotographic procedure. I.F.D., 14th Conference, Transactions, p. C135-C137, 1938.
73. Bendikson, L. Microfilms, as the first step in documentary photography. I.F.D., 14th Conference, Transactions, p. C129, 1938. Also published in F.I.D., Communicationes, 6 [1]:23-25, 1939.
74. Schürmeyer, W. Die vorteile der filmphotokopie. Zentralblatt für bibliothekswesen, 55:494-499, 1938.
75. Danton, J. Periam. Microphotography in a university library. Journal of documentary reproduction, I: 297-315, 1938.
76. Beveridge, R. A. [A critique of the above article]. Journal of documentary reproduction, II:166-168, 1939.

77. Danton, J. Periam. [An answer to the above critique]. Journal of documentary reproduction, II:221-224, 1939.
78. Jenkinson, Hilary and Sayce, Leonard A. Some notes on the application of microphotography to archives. I.F.D., 14th Conference, Transaction, p. C156-C157, 1938.
79. Fussler, H. H. American microphotography at the Paris exposition. American library association, Bulletin, 32:104-106, 1938.
80. U. S. Library of Congress, Report of the librarian of Congress for for the fiscal year ending June 30, 1939, Washington, D. C., 1939, p. 312.
81. Page, B. S. The organization of microphotography in Great Britain, I. F. D., 14th Conference, Transactions, p. C137-C138, 1938.
82. Leroy, Emile. La development du microfilm en France. F.I.D., 14th Conference, Transactions, p. C138-C141, 1938.
83. Raney, M. L. American trends in textual reproduction. F.I.D., Communicationes, VI [3]:C75-C79, 1939.
84. Power, E. B. Microfilm in Europe, 1939. Journal of documentary reproduction, II:254-258, 1939.
85. Sayce, L. A. Microphotography in 1939. Association of special libraries and information bureaux, Proceedings, 16:77-83, 1939.
86. Rogers, David G. Micro-film development. Special libraries, 31:235-237, 1940.
87. Jackson, William A. Some limitations of microfilm. Bibliographical society of America, Papers, 35:281-288, 1941.
88. Danton, J. Periam and Charles Elfont. Microphotography at work. Journal of documentary reproduction, 1:97-108, 1938.
89. Seidell, Atherton. The place of microfilm copying in library organization. Science, 94:114, 1941.
90. Edsall, Preston W. The file microcopy of the national archives. Journal of documentary reproduction, 4: 9, 1941.
91. U. S. Library of Congress, Report of the librarian of Congress for the fiscal year ending June 30, 1943, Washington, D. C., 1943, p. 193.
92. Greenwood, Herbert W. Document photography including copying and mass recording. London, 1943.
93. Mehne, E. Archivarische forderungen an die photomikrographische dokumentation von zeitdokumenten. Deutsche gesellschaft für dokumentation, Die dokumentation und ihre probleme, Leipzig, 1943, p. 176-179.

94. Rahts, W. Die photochemischen hilfsmittel für die dokumentation. Deutsche gesellschaft für dokumentation, Die dokumentation und ihre probleme, Leipzig, 1943, p. 180-189.
95. U. S. Library on Congress, Report of the librarian of Congress for the fiscal year ending June 30, 1944, Washington, D. C., 1944, p. 151.
96. De Sola, R. Microfilming. New York, 1944.
97. Moholy, L. Developments and extensions in the uses of microfilm. Association of special libraries and information bureaux, 19th Conference, Report of proceedings, p. 61-64, 1944.
98. Metcalf, Keyes D. Implications of microfilm and microprint for libraries. Library journal, 70:718-723, 1945.
99. Moholy, Lucia. A few remarks on documentary reproduction in general and microfilm in particular. Journal of documentation, 1:31-35, 1945-46.
100. Bush, Vannevar. As we may think. Atlantic monthly, 176:101-108, 1945. Reprinted in his: Endless horizons. Washington, D. C., 1946, p. 16-38.
101. Saint Rat, L. de. Le microfilm dans la vie pratique. F.I.D., Communicationes, 13 [4]:C55-C60, 1946.
102. Tate, Vernon D. Documentary reproduction--post war. Inter-American library conference, Papers and addresses, Washington, D. C., 1946, p. 17-23.
103. Moholy, Lucia. Aslib microfilm service, the story of the wartime activities. Journal of documentation, 2: 147-173, 1946.
104. Moholy, Lucia. Co-ordination of policy in documentary reproduction. F.I.D., Communicationes, 13 [4]:C60-, 1946.
105. United States War Department, Records administration, microfilming of records. Washington, D. C., 1946. (War Department, Technical Manual TM12-257)
106. Moholy, Lucia. Documentary reproduction. Nature, (London), 157:38-40, 1946. A condensation and revision of the same article retitled A central office of documentary reproduction was published in Royal Society, Empire scientific conference, Report, 1948, p. 717-721.
107. Redepenning, Wilhelm. Über probleme der lesefilmtechnik. Zentralblatt für bibliothekswesen, (Leipzig), 61:121-128, 1947.
108. Siedentopf, H. and J. Siedentopf. Dokumentation durch mikrokopie. Physikalische blätter, 3:267-270, 1947.
109. Downs, Robert B. Many study photography processes.

Library journal, 72:1649-1652, 1947.
110. Tate, Vernon D. From Binkley to Bush. American archivist, 10:249-257, 1947.
111. Power, Eugene B. University microfilms--a microfilming service for scholars. Journal of documentation, 2:23-31, 1946-47.
112. Forsdyke, Sir John. Some technical aspects of the production and use of microfilm. Museum journal (London), 48-184-186, 1948.
113. Emery, Alden H. The ACS photocopying service. Chemical and engineering news, 26, no. 20, p. 1437-7, 1948.
114. Jolley, Leonard. The use of microfilm for completing sets. Journal of documentation, 4:41-43, 1948-49.
115. Fielstra, Gerritt E. Photoreproduction of maps: practical? Library journal, 75:464-465, 1950.
116. Tate, Vernon D. An appraisal of microfilm. American documentation, 1:91-99, 1950.
117. Power, Eugene B. The use of high reduction microfilm in libraries. American documentation, 1:139-143, 1950.
118. Saint Rat, L. de. Exposition du microfilm et de la photocopie; memento technique. Paris, 1950.
119. Van der Wolk, L. J. and J. G. Tonnon. The microcopy on flat film as an aid in documentation (I-II). Revue de documentation, 17 [5]:134-141, 216-238, 1950.
120. Unesco, Microphotography; report of an enquiry concerning microphotography in countries other than the U. S. of Am.; assignment conducted by H. R. Verry. n.p., 1951. Mimeographed. Part II; report of an enquiry concerning methods and equipment for microphotography of the U. S. of Am. n.p., 1951. Mimeographed. (A summary of the first part, which appeared in 1950, is listed under no. 212 in this bibliography.)
121. Rider, Fremont. The possible correlation of all forms of microtext. American documentation, 2:152-157, 1951.
122. Wood, James L. Recommended microfilming practices, procedures and equipment, 1951, 76 f. Unpublished Master's Project, School of Library Science, Western Reserve University. Typewritten.
123. Bauhuis, W. Einiges zum mikrofilm hier und in U.S.A. Nachrichten für wissenschaftlichen bibliotheken, 5:80-85, 1952.
124. Born, Lester K. A synthesis on "microfilm" at the Library of Congress. Journal of documentation, 8:1-13,

1952.
125. Coblans, H. Some recent developments in microcopy. South African libraries, 19:77-81, 1952.
126. Spohr, Otto H. Photographische dokumente; ihre herstellung und verwendungsmöglichkeiten. Nachrichten für dokumentation, 3:108-114, 1952.
127. Federation international de documentation, Manual on document reproduction and selection, The Hague, 1953, 2 v.
128. Spohr, Otto H. Some recent developments in photographic documentation. South African libraries, 20:129-132, 1953.
129. Born, Lester K. Microfilm activity in Italy. U. S. Library of Congress information bulletin, 12:3, 25, May, 1953.
130. Randall, F. S. Microcosmos. Serial slants, 5:122-129, 1954.
131. Fussler, Herman H. Photographic reproduction of research materials. Library trends, 2:532-544, 1954.
132. Tate, Vernon D. Microreproduction and the acquisitions program. Library trends, 3:432-447, 1955.
133. Holmes, Donald C. Photoduplication at the Library of Congress. National micro-news, no. 7, Nov./Dec. 1954, unpaged.
134. Born, Lester K. Some animadversions on European standards and practices. American documentation, 5: 160-162, 1954.
135. National microfilm association, Committee on terminology, A glossary of microfilm terms (preliminary edition), National micro-news, no. 3, Feb./Mar. 1954, unpaged.
136. Ten Eyck, Hendrix. Glossary of terms used in microreproduction. Hingham, Mass., 1955.
137. Ballou, H. W. Microcopying methods and use. Doss, M. P., ed., Information processing equipment, New York, 1955, p. 67-104.
138. American Library Association, Committee on photoduplication and multiple copying methods, A guide to microfilming practices. National micro-news, no. 10, March, 1955, unpaged. Also issued as a separate, 18 p., mimeographed.
139. Webb, T., Jr. Microcopy, near print and the new film composing machines. Library quarterly, 25:111-124, 1955.
140. Integrated micrographic system. American documentation, 6:175-177, 1955.
141. Cain, A. Microfilming--the situation today. Aslib,

Proceedings, 7:23-30, 1955.
142. Lewis, C. M. The Times microfilm program. National micro-news, no. 14, July, 1955, unpaged.
143. Lewis, C. M. and W. H. Offenhauser, Jr. Microrecording; industrial and library applications, New York, 1956.
144. Henebry, A. Preservation of photographs on microfilm. Special libraries, 47:451-454, 1956.
145. Hermann, I. A. Manual of office reproduction. New York, 1956.
146. Bobb, F. W. Microfilm in a records management program. National micro-news, no. 26, p. 1-13, Oct., 1956.
147. Tate, Vernon D. Microcopy, nearprint and other reproduction processes. Special libraries, 47:461-463, 1956.
148. Ballou, H. W. Photography and the library. Library trends, 5:265-293, 1956.
149. Varden, L. E. Current trends in document copying. Industrial photography, 6:44-52, Feb., 1957.
150. McDonald, J. The case against microfilming. American archivist, 20:345-356, 1957.
151. Stevens, G. W. W. Microphotography; photography at extreme resolution. New York, 1957. Especially chapter 12, Document microphotography.
152. Cinescopie. London University, Institute of historical research, Bulletin, 7:168-169, 1930.
153. Allen, C. B. Focusing device for copying with small cameras. Camera (Philadelphia), 47:100-103, 1933.
154. Björkbom, Carl. Stockholm's new photographic apparatus. Library journal, 58:316, 1933.
155. Ficklen, J. B. Copying manuscripts on motion picture film. Science, 80:210, 1934.
156. McKay, H. C. Practical copying procedure. Miniature camera, 2:223-227, 1934.
157. Leitz, E. Emploi d'un petit appareil à pellicules pour la reproduction de documents. Scientific and industrial photography, ser. 2, 6:389, 1935.
158. Seidell, Atherton. Les derniers progrès de la photographie des documents sur film. Office international de chimie, La utilisation du film comme support de la documentation, Paris, 1935, p. 47-52.
159. Schürmeyer, W. Der "Rollofot" ein photokopiergerat. Zentralblatt für bibliothekswesen (Leipzig), 52:216-218, 1935.
160. Kellner, G. W. A combined enlarging and projecting equipment with reading desk. I.I.D., Communicationes,

3 [1]:Kel-4, 1936.
161. New projection printer. Journal of documentary reproduction, 1:279, 1938.
162. Binkley, Robert C. The camera. American library association, Microphotography for libraries, Chicago, 1936, p. 3-9.
163. Draeger, Rupert H. Some technical aspects of microphotography. Society of motion picture engineers, Journal, 27:84-89, 1936.
164. Draeger, Rupert H. Photographic emulsions and media in microphotography. American library association, Microphotography for libraries, Chicago, 1936, p. 10-12.
165. Raney, M. L. The microphotographic camera. American library association, Bulletin, 31:211-213, 1937.
166. Seidell, Atherton. A new camera for microfilm photography in libraries. Congrès mondial de documentation universelle, 1937, La documentation..., 1937, p. 308-310.
167. Saint Rat, L. de. Microphotocopies et microthèques. I.I.D., Communicationes, 4 [1]:21-24, 1937.
168. Folmer-Graflex Corporation, Graflex Photorecord manual, Rochester, 1937.
169. Draeger, R. H. A new design for the microphotographic camera. Congrès mondial de la documentation universelle, 1937, La documentation..., 1937, p. 62-63.
170. Draeger, R. H. The Paris mechanisms I: the camera. American library association, Microphotography for libraries, 1937, Chicago, 1937, p. 39-40.
171. Bendikson, L. Miniature camera in library work. Photographic journal, 77:269-271, 1937.
172. Macalpine, G. B. Miniature camera in library work. Photographic journal, 77:313, 1937.
173. Fussler, Herman H. New microphotographic laboratory is established at Chicago. American library association, Bulletin, 31:295-297, 1937.
174. Fussler, Herman H. Microphotography for smaller libraries. American library association, Bulletin, 31: 4-42, 1937.
175. Johnson, Amandus. Some early experiences in microphotography 1910-1938. Journal of documentary reproduction, 1:9-19, 1938.
176. Kerrins, J. Q. The record registry camera. Journal of documentary reproduction, 1:279, 1938.
177. Technical description of new microbook method of high-reduction microfilm book making. Journal of docu-

mentary reproduction, 1:279, 1938.
178. Holbrook, J. K. The Holbrook microfilming camera. Journal of documentary reproduction, 1:221-223, 1938.
179. Draeger newspaper camera in operation. Journal of documentary reproduction, 1:276, 1938.
180. Stauffer, Alvin P. Microphotography in the National Park Service. Journal of documentary reproduction, 1:152-161, 1938.
181. Raney, M. L. The decision of Paris. Journal of documentary reproduction, 1:152-161, 1938.
182. The present status of equipment and supplies for microphotography. Journal of documentary reproduction, 1, no. 3, pt. 2, 1938.
183. Haughton, Sidney H. Preservation of records by microphotography in the United States of America. Journal of documentation, 1:156-161, 1938.
184. Library photography. Library journal, 63:377, 1938.
185. Technical and news notes. Journal of documentary reproduction, 1:82-83, 1938. This column appears also in later issues.
186. Automatic paper printer developed. Journal of documentary reproduction, 1:340, 1938.
187. Fussler, Herman H. The mechanization of microphotographic equipment. F.I.D., Communicationes, 6: 25, 1939.
188. Raney, M. L. Microphotographic equipment. American archivist, 2:145-153, 1939.
189. Flemer, H. I. The new S.R.S. camera. Journal of documentary reproduction, 2:225, 1939.
190. Fussler, Herman H. Library photography. Library journal, 64:556, 1939.
191. Fussler, Herman H. Library photography, Library journal, 64:279, 1939.
192. Fussler, Herman H. Library photography. Library journal, 64:151, 1939.
193. Rahts, W. Neuere photo-materialien fuer die dokumentation. F.I.D., Communicationes, 6 [3]:127-128. A translation by I. O. Garodnick was published in Journal of documentary reproduction, 3:216-219, 1940.
194. Boeing, John K. Recordak. Journal of documentary reproduction, 3:153-168, 1940.
195. Fussler, Herman H. A new microfilm printer. Journal of documentary reproduction, 3:92-95, 1940.
196. Worth, John T. Microphotography with a Rolleicord camera. Journal of documentary reproduction, 3:247-251, 1940.
197. Reid, J. D. Microfilm with the 35-millimeter candid

camera. Science, n.s., 91:555-556, 1940.
198. Tate, Vernon D. Recordak microfilm enlarger. Journal of documentary reproduction, 4:252-253, 1941.
199. Fussler, Herman H. Photographic reproduction for libraries. Chicago, 1942.
200. Library of Congress, Report of the librarian of Congress for the fiscal year ending June 30, 1944, Washington, D. C., 1944, 204 p.
201. Library of Congress, Report of the librarian of Congress for the fiscal year ending June 30, 1947. Washington, D. C., 1947, 181 p.
202. Van Alphen, P. M., and C. J. Dippel. New technical possibilities in the microreproduction and multiplication of documents. F. I. D., 17th Conference, Rapports, 1:75-78, 1947.
203. Dippel, C. J. and K. J. Kenning. Problems in photographic reproduction, in particular of sound films. Philips technical review, 9:65-72, 1947/48.
204. Alink, R. J. and others. The metal-diazonium system for photographic reproduction. Philips technical review, 9:289-300, 1947/48.
205. Oosterloo, N. The direct possibilities of microphotography. Revue de la documentation, 16 [3]:80-83, 1949.
206. Taubes, Ernest P. Microfilm camera records both sides of documents. Electrical Manufacturing (New York, 41:76-80, 166, 168, 170, 1948.)
207. Bobb, Frank W. Applying microfilm in a war agency. Special libraries, 39:50-52, 1948.
208. Schürmeyer, W. Die Leica im dienst der bibliotheken und der dokumentation. Stöckler, der Leica in benif und wissenschaft, Frankfort, 1949, p. 159-172.
209. Taube, Mortimer. New tools for the control and use of research materials. American philosophical society, Proceedings, 96:251-2, 1949.
210. Van Santen, J. J. M. De reproductieschuif. Documentatie reproductie, 2:53-56, 76-79, 1949.
211. Anderson, H. A. A new Swedish reproduction camera. Tidskrift för dokumentation, vol. 6, 1950.
212. Verry, H. R. Unesco survey of microfilm use--1950. Unesco bulletin for libraries, 5:161-167, 1951.
213. Bastardie, J. J. Microcopying supplement no. 1. Unesco bulletin for libraries, 6:F32-E35, B14-B22, 1952.
214. Bastardie, J. J. Microcopying supplement no. 2. Unesco bulletin for libraries, 6E76-79, B52-59, 1952. (This and the preceding item were issued under

one cover as a separate.)
215. Janicki, W. Recent Swiss apparatus for microfilm reading and photocopying. Revue de la documentation, 18 [3]:135-140, 1951.
216. Reichelt, Werner. Technische helfsmittel der mikrodocumentation. Nachrichten für dokumentation, 2:12-13, 1951.
217. Offenhauser, William E., Jr. Preservation by microfilm. Special libraries, 42:369-373, 397-400, 1951.
218. Knigge, Hans J. Phototechnische nachrichten im dienste der dokumentation. Nachrichten für dokumentation, 3:91-94, 1952.
219. U. S. Library of Congress, Report of the librarian for the fiscal year ending June 30, 1952, Washington, D. C., 1952, 192 p.
220. Welp, V. Weache eigenschaften mussen hochwertige dokumentfilme besitzen. Nachrichten für dokumentation, 5:39-41, 1954.
221. Hornung, Walter. Neue photomaterialien für die dokumentenreproduktion. DFW, 3:17-19, 1954.
222. Gibson, Thomas and Archibald L. Goodall. An inexpensive apparatus for microfilm reproductions. Medical library association, Bulletin, 42:328-331, 1954.
223. Reed, F. C. Copy stand used in making microfilm negatives of books. Biological photographers association, Journal, 22:161-164, 1954.
224. U. S. Library of Congress, Report of the librarian of Congress for the fiscal year ending June 30, 1954, Washington, D. C., 1954, p. 87.
224a. Léauté, J. Supports transparents "de sécurité," pour microcopies, Courrier de normalisation, année 22, p. 141-147, 1955.
224b. Guillot, G. Les realisations des constructeurs français. Courrier de normalisation, année 22, p. 148-158, 1955.
225. Peckinpaugh, C. L., Jr. An automatic processor for instrumentation film. Photographic engineering, 7: 147, 156, 1956.
226. Kiersky, Loretta J. Recent developments in photoreproduction. Special libraries, 47:328-329, 464-465, 1956; 48:103-104, 1957.
227. Flemer, H. L. and Atherton Seidell. The FS microfilm camera. American documentation, 8:127, 1957.
228. Holloway, Jack. The Paris mechanisms II. American library association, Microphotography for libraries, 1937, Chicago, 1937, p. 40-44.
229. Microfilm printer acquired by American documentation

institute. Journal of docu mentary reproduction, 1: 276, 1938.
230. Jenkinson, Hilary and Leonard A. Sayce. Some notes on the application of microphotography to archives. F.I.D., 14th Conference, Transactions, 1:C156-C157, 1938.
231. Saint Rat, L. de. Application du microfilm à la photographie de luminescence. F.I.D., 14th Conference, Transactions, 1:C153-C155, 1938.
232. Fussler, Herman H. Use of light filters in microphotography. Library journal, 65:43, 1940.
233. Noll, Daniel F. Exposure in microphotography. Journal of documentary reproduction, 4:244-251, 1941.
234. Crabtree, J. I., G. T. Eaton and L. E. Muehler. The elimination of hypo from photographic images. Society of motion picture engineers, Journal, 35:484-506, 1940. Also published in American photography, p. 272-285, 1941.
235. Garver, George Thomas, Jr. Use of microfilm in the library of the American philosophical society. Special libraries, 33:76-78, 1942.
236. Stevens, G. W. W. Some practical aspects of microphotography. Photographic journal, 84:108-111, 1944.
237. Tritton, F. J. Additional uses for 35 mm. microcopying film (extremely fine grain and resolving power). British journal of photography, 93:374, 1946.
238. Boon, S. D. Grenzen bij de microdocumentatie van teekeningen. Document reproductie, 2:20-22, 1949.
239. Ashworth, Wilford. Photographic technique in library work. Librarian, 40:32-26, 1951.
240. Weigert, K. M. Some photographic copying methods useful in libraries. Photographic science and technique, 2:79-80, 1955.

General

241. Seidell, Atherton. Filmstats, a new method for the advancement of science. Journal of chemical education, 12:415-418, 1935.
242. Umbreit, W. La copie des documents sur films et la copie directe sur papier. Office international de chimie, L'Utilisation du film comme support de la documentation, Paris, 1935, p. 2-14.
243. Raney, M. L. Microphotography: a lay appraisal. Journal of documentary reproduction, 1:20-32, 1938.
244. Royal society, Scientific information conference, Report and papers submitted, London, 1948.

245. Tauber, Maurice. Problems in the use of microfilms, microprint and microcards in research libraries. Industrial and engineering chemistry, 42:1467-1468, 1950.
246. Shoemaker, R. J. Remarks on microcards and microfilms for newspapers. American documentation, 1: 207-208, 1950.
247. Ballou, Hubbard W. and J. Rather. Microfilm and microfacsimile publication. Library trends, 4:182-194, 1955.
248. Shaw, Ralph R. Publication and distribution of scientific literature. College and research libraries, 17: 293-303, 1956.

Microfilm

249. Page, B. S., L. A. Sayce and E. F. Patterson. Microphotography: standards in "format", storage and cataloguing. Library association record, 40:212-216, 1938. The same material with some augmentation was published in F.I.D., 14th Conference, Transactions, 1:141-146, 1938.
250. Wilson, H. E. The ten-page strip. Federation international de documentation, 17th Conference, Rapports, 1:83-84, 1947.
251. Power, Eugene B. Factors influencing the cost of microfilm. Federation international de la documentation, 17th Conference, Rapports, 1:79-82, 1947.
252. A new project, the Library of Congress. Special libraries, 39:29, 1948.
253. Power, Eugene B. Symposium on microreproduction: microfilm. Serial slants, 3:43-46, 1952.
254. New developments in microreproduction. Special libraries, 48:149, 1957.

Sheet microfilm

255. Bennett, Ralph D. Sheet film. Journal of documentary reproduction, 3:39-41, 1940. The full findings of the investigation enumarized in this paper were apparently not published.
256. Reyniers, James A., P. C. Trexler, and R. F. Ervin. The use of flat film for microcopy. Journal of documentary reproduction, 4:3-8, 1941.
257. Redepenning, Wilhelm. Stand der praktischen mikrokopie. Physikalische blätter, 4:299-301, 1948.
258. Van der Wolk, L. J., and J. C. Tonnon. La micro-

fiche en documentation. Hommes et techniques, 9:67-73, 1953.
259. Riehl, G. Documentation et archives: les microfiches et microcartes. Hommes et techniques, 9:149-152, 1953.
260. Power, E. B. The use of sheet film for newspaper clippings. Special libraries, 44:111-114, 1954.
261. Mink, Henri de. Mikrobladed-en-ny mojlighet vid mikrofotografering. Tidskrift für dokumentation, 12(6): 69-72, 1956.

Composite forms

262. Seidell, Atherton. Photomicrographic reproduction of documents. I.I.D., Communicationes, 1 [3]:22-25, 1934. The same article was published in Science, 80:184-185, 1934.
263. Salchow, W. Karteikarte met losen kleinbildern oder film. I.I.D., Communicationes, 3 [1]:col. sa. 1-2, 1936.
264. A new type of lantern slide.... Journal of documentary reproduction, 1:183, 1938.
265. Williams, Theodore J. and A. Rose. A solution to the problem of storage and availability of chemical literature. Journal of chemical education, 29:146-147, March, 1952.
266. Kard-a-film, Library journal 77:203, 1952.
267. Batchelder, R. W. Unit filing of microfilm widens its applications. National micro-news, no. 20, (unpaged), February, 1956.
268. Tyler, A. W., W. L. Myers, and J. W. Kuipers. The application of the Kodak Minicard system to problems of documentation. American documentation, 6:18-30, 1955.
269. Reed, Eugene B. A coded geologic data file on microsheets. National micro-news, no. 28, (unpaged), December, 1956.

Micropaper

270. Bendikson, L. Some photochemical methods for the preservation and restoration of documents. Library journal, 60:745-6, 1935. The same article appears in I.I.D., Communicationes, 3 [1]:col. Be 1-6, 1936.
271. Bendikson, L. Contact prints of microfilms. Congrès mondial de la documentation universelle, 1937, Texte des communicationes, p. 21.

272. Van Iterson, G. An improved method for preparing and reading reproduction on a reduced scale of scientific communications, 8 [3]:43-46, 1941.

Microcards

273. Union catalogs at low cost. Journal of documentary reproduction, 2:62, 1938.
274. Rider, Fremont. The scholàr and the future of the research library. Hadham Press, 1944.
275. Rider, Fremont. The promise of microprint, a symposium based on The scholar and the future of the research library. College and research libraries, 6: 170-183, 1945.
276. Rider, Fremont. Progress in microprint: part I, microcards--the next steps. College and research libraries, 6:429-440, 1945.
277. Progress in microprint: part II, the microcard code. College and research libraries, 6:441-446, 1945.
278. Besterman, Theodore. (Review of Rider, The scholar and the future of the research library), Journal of documentary reproduction, 1:57-59, 1945/46.
279. Moholy, Lucia. (Review of Rider, The scholar...). Journal of documentary reproduction, 1:59-61, 1945/46.
280. Sayce, L. A. (Review of Rider, The scholar...). Journal of documentary reproduction, 1:61-62, 1945/46.
281. The microcard project. Journal of documentation, 1: 162-163, 1945/46.
282. Microcard bulletin, 1948.
283. Price, Miles. Microcards vs. micro-film and microprint. Microcard bulletin, 2:1, 1948.
284. Parsonage, S. J. "The scholar" and after; a study of the development of the microcard. Library association record (London), 51:334-338, 1949.
284a. Keenleyside, Marjorie C. Microcards and the special library, 40:92-94, 1949.
285. Microcard production gets underway. Library journal, 73:361, 1949.
286. Kuipers, J. W. Microcards and microfilm for a central reference file. Industrial and engineering chemistry, 42:1463-1467, 1950.
287. Rider, Fremont. Microcards, a new form of publication. Industrial and engineering chemistry, 42:1462-1463, 1950.
288. Rider, Fremont. Archival materials on microcards. American documentation (Washington), 1:42-45, 1950.
289. Rider, Fremont. Warehouse or "Microcard"? Library

journal, 75:pt. 1, p. 832-836, pt. 2, p. 927-931, 1950.
290. Kuipers, J. W. Microcards and documentation. American documentation, (Washington), 2:89-95, 1951.
291. Verry, H. R. Micro-opaques. Aslib proceedings, 4: 153-162, 1952.

Microtape and microstrip

292. Baptie, Alex L. Microtape. National micro-news, no. 7, (unpaged), 1947.
293. New product for unit filing of micro-images. National micro-news, no. 4, (unpaged), 1954.

Readex Microprint

294. Fussler, Herman H. Library photography. Library journal, 64:191, 1939.
295. Readex microprint. Journal of documentary reproduction, 2:175, 1939.
296. American library association, Photographic reproduction of library materials committee. American library association bulletin, 33:657-658, 1939.
297. Tennant, John. Readex microprints. Journal of documentary reproduction, 3:66-70, 1940.
298. Raney, M. L. Microprint. Journal of documentary reproduction, 4:94, 1941.
299. Boni, Albert. Microprint. American documentation, 2:150-152, 1951.
300. Erickson, Edgar L. Microprint: a revolution in printing. Journal of documentation, 7:184-187, 1951.

Microlex

301. Knight, E. G. The miracle of microlex--a new kind of lawbook. Case and comment, 60:3-7, 1955.

Lithoprinting in miniature

302. Champlin, Carol D. Lithoprinting in miniature. Congrès mondial de la documentation universelle, 1937, La documentation..., Paris, 1937, p. 58-61.
303. Edwards, J. W. Lithoprinting for reproducing research materials in limited-copy editions. Journal of documentation, 2:32-34, 1946-47.

Micrometal

304. Carter, Robert W. Metalfilm for permanent records. Journal of documentary reproduction, 1:354-361, 1938.
305. Peters, T. K. Records for the future. Journal of documentary reproduction, 1:168-171, 1938.

General

306. Case, C. Z. Quality and costs in textual filming. F.I.D., Communicationes, 6 [3]:C88-C95, 1939, (International federation for documentation, 16th Conference).
307. Holmes, Donald C. Quality in microphotography. Journal of documentary reproduction, 2:284-285, 1939.
308. [Minimum standards of quality for permanent record microfilms]. Journal of documentary reproduction, 4: 230-231, 1941.
309. Flemer, H. L. Assaying the developer. Journal of documentary reproduction, 5:142-145, 1942.
310. Higgins, G. C., and L. A. Jones. The nature and evaluation of the sharpness of photographic images. Society of motion picture engineers, Journal, 55:277-290, 1952.
311. Verry, H. R. Colour response in document reproduction processes. Great Britain, Treasury, O. & M. Bulletin, 8:no. 4, 43-45, 1953.
312. Rudd, R. G. Some factors influencing the quality of microfilm images. National microfilm association, Proceedings, second annual meeting, 1953, p. 44-58, 1953.
313. Clapp, Verner H., Francis H. Henshaw, Donald C. Holmes. Are your microfilms deteriorating acceptably? Library journal, 80:588-595, 1955.
314. U. S. Library of Congress, Report of the librarian for the fiscal year ending June 30, 1955, Washington, D. C., 1955.
315. Van Gieson, J. E. Quality of microfilm images as affected by film and developer characteristics. National microfilm association, Proceedings, fifth annual meeting, 1956, p. 81-87, 1956.

Reduction ratios

316. Sayce, Leonard A. Standardisation in microphotography. Federation international de documentation, 14th Conference, Transactions, 1938, p. 141-a revision of the paper listed as 215.
317. Townsend, Agnes. Resolving power in microcopying.

Journal of documentary reproduction, 2:140-146, 1939.
318. Lubeck, Heinz. Grundsätzliche fragen des mikrobuches. Zentralblatt für bibliothekswesen, 63:17-29, 1949.
319. Shaw, Ralph R. Management, machines, and the bibliographic problems of the twentieth century. Shera, Jesse H. and Margaret E. Egan, Bibliographic organization; papers presented before the fifteenth annual conference of the Graduate Library School, July 24-29, 1950, Chicago, 1951, p. 200-225.
320. American library association. Committee on photoduplication. Quality loss in newspaper microfilm. American documentation, 2:112-113, 1951.

Residual hypo

321. Crabtree, J. I. and J. F. Ross. A method of testing for the presence of sodium thiosulfate in motion picture films. Society of motion picture engineers, Journal, 14:419, 1930.
322. Gibson, James E., and Charles G. Weber. The evaluation of motion picture films by semimicro testing. Journal of documentary reproduction, 1:282-288, 1938.
323. Fussler, Herman H. Library photography. Library journal, 65:207, 1940.
324. Fussler, Herman H. Library photography. Library journal, 65:203, 1940.
325. Fussler, Herman H. Library photography. Library journal, 66:213, 405, 1941.
326. American standards association. American standard method for predicting the permanency of the silver images of procedded films, plates and papers, Z38.8.17-1948, New York, 1948. Now superseded by its American standard method for indicating the stability of the images of processed black-and-white films, plates, and papers, P114.12-1954, New York, 1954.
327. American standards association. American standard method for determining residual thiosulfate and tetrathionate in processed photographic papers, Z38.8.25-1950, New York, 1950.

Durability and stability

328. Scribner, B. W. National bureau of standards research on stability of filmslides. American library association, Microphotography for libraries, 1936, Chicago, 1936, p. 44-46. Also published in American library association, Public documents committee, Public doc-

uments, 1936, p. 207-209.

329. Hill, John R. and Charles G. Weber. Stability of motion picture films as determined by accelerated aging. National bureau of standards, Journal of research, 17:871-81, 1936. (National bureau of standards research paper 950). Also published in Society of motion picture engineers, Journal, 27:677-690.

330. Hill, John R. and Charles G. Weber. Evaluation of motion-picture film for permanent records. National bureau of standards, Misc. publ. M158, Washington, D. C., 1937.

331. Kimberley, A. E., and B. W. Scribner. Summary report of the National bureau of standards research on preservation of records. National bureau of standards, Misc. publ. 154, Washington, D. C., 1937.

332. Scribner, B. W. Notes on selection of cellulose acetate film for record purposes. Journal of documentary reproduction, 1:209-211, 1938.

333. Clement, L. and C. Riviere. Résultats de la conservation d'acétates de cellulose, de nitroacétates de cellulose et de films de celluloid or de sûreté apres 25 annees. Congrès de chimie industrielle, 18me Congrès, 1938, Compte rendu, p. 703-717.

334. Scribner, B. W. Summary report of research at the National bureau of standards on the stability and preservation of records on photographic film. U. S. national bureau of standards, Misc. publ. M162, Washington, D. C., 1939.

335. U. S. national bureau of standards, Standard for permanent record photographic microcopying film (gelatin-silver halide emulsion type). Journal of documentary reproduction, 5:243, 1942.

336. Würstlin, K. A few requirements for the durability of microfilm, standards and terminology. Nachrichten für dokumentation, 2:59-61, 1951.

Standards and terminology

337. Symposium sur l'utilization du film en matière de documentation. I.I.D., Communicationes, 2:[3]:Col 57-59, 1935.

338. U. S. national bureau of standards. Photographic film for miniature copies of records, simplified practice recommendation R165-36, effective date Aug. 1, 1938, Washington, D. C., 1936.

339. Tate, Vernon D. Microphotography at Zurich. Journal of documentary reproduction, 2:259-264, 1939.

340. Bobb, Frank W. Microfilm standards. Special libraries, 33:325-328, 1942.
341. American standards association. American standard for films for permanent records, Z38.3.2-1945. New York, 1945.
342. American standards association. American standard practice for microfilms, Z38.7.8-1947. New York, 1947.
343. British standards institution. British standards specifications, 1947, no. 1371. London, 1947.
344. Association of research libraries, Committee on the photographic reproduction of research materials. A proposed standard for the microphotographic reproduction of newspapers. American documentation, 1: 46-50, 1950.
345. Eighteenth international congress of the international federation for documentation. Unesco bulletin for libraries, 6:E3, 1952.
346. Microfilms and microcards; standardization for documentary reproduction. Unesco bulletin for libraries, 6:E108, 1952.
347. To improve standards for photographic reproduction. Library journal, 78:1509-1510, 1953.
348. Clapp, V. W. Standards in photographic reproduction of documents. Library of Congress information bulletin, 12:no. 21, 12-13.
349. Frontard, R. Present position and prospects of international standardization in the field of microcopying. Unesco bulletin for libraries, 8:suppl. Ei-Eviii, 1954. A French translation containing some later information was published in: Courrier de normalisation, année 22, p. 177-182, 1955.
350. Duyvis, F. Donker. Standardization as a tool of scientific management. Library trends, 2:410-427, 1954.
351. Martijn, J. Microfilm en samenwerking. Bibliotheek gids, 30:145-146, 1954.
352. Standards. National micro-news, no. 17, [unpaged], Nov., 1955.
353. [Numéro spécial "microcopie"]. Courrier de la normalisation, no. 122, Mar./April, 1955.
354. Holmes, Donald C. Photographic standards activities in U.S.A. and abroad. National microfilm association, Proceedings, p. 25-41, 1956.
355. Progress report on the bibliofilm service. U. S. Department of Agriculture, Agricultural library notes, 10:241-242, 1935.
356. Schellenberg, T. R. Library applications of microcopy-

ing. Library journal, 60:289-292, 1935.
357. Metcalf, Keyes D. The need for planning in microphotography. American library association, Microphotography for libraries, 1936, Chicago, 1936, p. 35-43.
358. Binkley, Robert C. Techniques and policies of documentary reproduction. I.F.D., 14th Conference, Transactions, 1:C121-C124, 1938. Also published in F.I.D. Communicationes, 6 [1]:12-15, 1939.
359. Bibliofilm service. Library journal, 63:902, 1938.
360. University of Chicago filming rates. Journal of documentary reproduction, 1:206-207, 1938.
361. Microfilming service at University of Michigan. Journal of documentary reproduction, 1:195, 1938.
362. Tilleux, Eugene Adhemar. Microphotography in 1940. Journal of documentary reproduction, 6:25-41, 1941.
363. Trivedi, M. C. Photocopying: its progress and equipment. Journal of documentary reproduction, 4:265-271, 1941.
364. Seidell, Atherton. The cost of microfilm copying in libraries. Journal of documentary reproduction, 6:164-167, 1941.
365. Worth, John T. (letter), Library journal, 66:319, 1941.
366. Shaw, Ralph R. Bibliofilm service of the U.S. Department of Agriculture library. Journal of documentary reproduction, 5:198-208, 1942.
367. Shaw, Ralph R. Continuous photoprinting at the USDA library. Library journal, 70:738-741, 1945.
368. Janicki, W. Cost estimating and cost analysis in reproduction work. F.I.D., Communicationes, 8 [3]: C30-C35, 1941.
369. Rider, F. Microcards. Medical library association, Bulletin, (Baltimore), 37:10-14, 1949.
370. Meeuwis, A. Een kostenvergelÿking van enige vermenigvuldigings en reproductiemiddelen. Document reproductie, 2:no. 3/4, 38-48, 1949.
371. Power, Eugene B. Microfilm as an edition process of documentary reproduction. American documentation, 2:157-166, 1951.
372. The cost of microfilm. Great Britain, Treasury, Organization and methods division, O & M bulletin, 8: no. 5, 34-39, 1953.
373. Masters, Betty R. The microfilming of records, with special reference to the work recently carried out at Exeter. Society of local archivists, Bulletin 11, Apr., 1953.
374. Fifield, Hugh S. An accounting system for a micro-

filming service company. National micro-news, no. 16, (unpaged), 1955.
375. Pritsker, Allan B. and J. William Sadler. An evaluation of microfilm as a method of book storage. College and research libraries, 18:290-296, 1957. Based on a M.S. thesis, the manuscript of which is on file in the library of the School of Engineering of Columbia University.
376. Crabtree, J. H. and H. C. Carlton. Cleaning fluids for motion picture film. Society of Motion Picture Engineers, Transactions, 11:277-293, 1927.
377. Weber, C. G. and J. R. Hill. Care of slide films and motion picture films in libraries. U. S. National bureau of standards, Journal of research, 17:753-769, 1936. Also published in Society of motion picture engineers, Journal, 27:691-702, 1936.
378. Raney, M. L. Film treatment. American library association, Bulletin, 30:894, 1936.
379. Metcalf, Keyes D. Care and cataloging of microfilms. American library association, Bulletin, 31:72-74, 1937.
380. Fox, Lewis J. Film for folios. Library journal, 62: 363, 1937.
381. Carruthers, Ralph H. and Wyllis E. Wright. Library methods of handling microfilm. American library association, Bulletin, 32:385-387, 1938.
382. Scribner, B. W. Summary report of research at the National bureau of standards on materials for the reproduction of records. F.I.D., Communicationes, 6 [1]:17-20, 1939.
383. Maurer, J. A. and W. Bach. The shrinkage of acetate base motion picture film. Society of motion picture engineers, Journal, 31:15-27, 1938.
384. Repairing and restoring microfilm. Journal of documentary reproduction, 1:343-344, 1938.
385. Metcalf, Keyes D. The preservation and service of textual film. F.I.D., Communicationes, 6 [1]:36-38, 1939.
386. Brown, H. F. and J. A. Austin. Simple method for the filing of microfilm records in short length strips. Science, 90:573-574, 1939.
387. Cibella, Rose C. Filing and cataloging of microfilms. Special libraries, 30:160-163, 1939.
388. Filclips for filing short lengths of microfilm. Journal of documentary reproduction, 2:56, 1939.
389. Jakes, F. Filing and preserving microfilm. Special libraries, 30:163-165, 1939.

390. Dice, L. R. A simple method for filing miniature negatives and microfilm records in strips. Science, 89:39-40, 1939.
391. Fussler, Herman H. Library photography, Library journal, 65:400, 1940.
392. Power, Eugene B. A microfilm storage cabinet. Journal of documentary reproduction, 3:96-98, 1940.
393. Globe-Wernicke microfilm storage cabinet. Journal of documentary reproduction, 4:56, 1941.
394. Society of motion picture engineers, Report of the Committee on preservation of motion picture film. Society of motion picture engineers. Journal, 35:584-606, 1940.
395. Lilley, Oliver L. Filing short length microfilms. Special libraries, 32:122-123, 133, 1941.
396. Microfilm storage file. Library journal, 66:271, 1941.
397. Eastmas Kodak Company. Storage of microfilms, sheet films and prints. Rochester, 1946.
398. British standards institution. British standard recommendations for the storage of microfilm, 1944, no. 1153. London, 1944. Superseded by British standard recommendations for the storage of microfilm, 1955. London, 1955.
399. Bacon, G. W. Handling microcards in libraries. College and research libraries, 11:372-272, 1950.
400. Noll, Daniel F. The maintenance of microfilm. American archivist, 13:129-134, 1950.
401. La conservation des microfilms. Cahiers, 8:102, 1951.
402. Great Britain, Public record office. Microphotography and archives. Archivum, 3:81-86, 1953.
403. Darling, R. H. The use of 70 mm. microfilm in safeguarding drawings. National microfilm association, Proceedings, p. 34-43, 1953.
404. Collison, R. L. Modern storage equipment and methods for special materials in libraries. Hampstead, 1955. Incorporated with changes in The treatment of special material in libraries, London, 1955.
405. Jacobson, T. Harold. [Report on maintenance of humidity in a Y & E microfilm file cabinet], National micro-news, no. 8, [unpaged], 1955.
406. Baumhofer, Hermine A. Film records management. American archivist, 19:235-248, 1956.
407. Weber, David C. How to store microfilm cheaply. Library journal, 81:1978-1980, 1956.
408. American standards association, PH5. A proposed standard for the storage of microfilm. National micro-news, no. 26, [unpaged], 1956.

409. Luecke, Camilla P. Photographic library procedures. Special libraries, 47:455-461, 1956.
410. Vanderbilt, P. Report on an experimental section of the proposed union library catalogue of the Philadelphia metropolitan area. I.I.D., Communicationes, 3 [3]:col. Va, 1-24, 1936.
411. Sébille, Georges. Vers le catalogue automatique par l'emploi des larges nappes de film. Congrès mondial de documentation universelle, 1937, La documentation..., 1937, p. 305-307.
412. Noll, Daniel F. Some recent developments in public record microfilming. Journal of documentary reproduction, 4:109, 1941.
413. Shaw, Ralph R. The Rapid Selector. Journal of documentation, 5:164-171, 1949.
414. Engineering Research Associates, Inc. Report for the Microfilm Rapid Selector. St. Paul, 1949.
415. U. S. Department of Commerce, Office of technical services, Instructions for the operation and maintenance of the Microfilm Rapid Selector, Washington, 1949, PB97313S. Processed.
416. Green, John C. The Rapid Selector--an automatic library. Revue de la documentation, 16 [3]:66-69, 1949.
417. New machine will scan, select and copy research data at high speed. Library journal, 13:797, 806, 1948.
418. Photoelectric librarian. Electronics, 22:122, 158, 160, 162, 164, 166, 1949.
419-420. Canovan, Ruth. Running a library for an engineering office. Engineering-news record, 143:32-35, 1949.
421. Shaw, Ralph R. High-speed intermittent camera. American documentation, 1:194-196, 1950.
422. Engstrom, H. T. Microfilm selection equipment in information work. Industrial and engineering chemistry, 42:1460-61, 1950.
423. Shaw, Ralph R. Machines and the bibliographical problems of the twentieth century. Bibliography in an age of science, Urbana, 1951, p. 37-71.
424. Vickery, Brian C. Some comments on mechanical selection. American documentation, 2:102-107, 1951.
425. Schulman, D. A. [Western Union Telegraph Company apparatus]. Electrical Manufacturing, 47:110-112, 1951.
426. Jamieson, D. R. Mechanized bibliographic aid. Library association record, 53:216-221, 1951.
427. Schürmeyer, Walther. Selecto-ein eues auswahlsystem für die dokumentation. Nachrichten für dokumentation, 3:33-34, 1952.

428. Knigge, H. J. Mikrofilm und lochkarte. Nachrichten für dokumentation, 3:125-128, 1952.
429. Samain, J. Filmorex; une nouvelle technique de classement et de selection des documents et des informations. Paris, 1952.
430. Filmorex system for electronic selection of microfilm cards. Unesco monthly circular, no. 7, p. 5-6, 1952.
431. Gull, C. D. Instrumentation. Library trends, 2:103-126, 1953.
432. Shaw, Ralph R. Rapid Selector patented. Library journal, 78:310, 1953.
433. Avakian, Emik A. and Eugene Garfield. AMFIS-the automatic microfilm information system. Special libraries, 48:145-148, 1957.
434. Literature notes. American documentation, 4:174-175, 1953.
435. Verry, H. R. Rapid selectors. Great Britain, Treasury, organization and methods division, O & M bulletin, 8:43-46, 1953.
436. Niven, Donald H. New photostat apparatus to enlarge and process from microfilm. National microfilm association, Proceedings, p. 11-15, 1954.
437. Shaw, Ralph R. The Rapid Selector. American institute of biological sciences, Bulletin, 4:20-21, 1954.
438. Shaw, Ralph R. Mechanical and electronic aid for bibliography. Library trends, 2:522-531, 1954.
439. An automatic microimage file searches film record and makes photographic print. National bureau of stanards, Technical news bulletin, 40:89-90, 1956.

Index

K

L

M

N

T

www.ingramcontent.com/pod-product-compliance
Ingram Content Group UK Ltd.
Pitfield, Milton Keynes, MK11 3LW, UK
UKHW020207290926
15470UKWH00001B/40

9 780837 182353